Student Success

How To Be a Better Student
and Still Have Time
For Your Friends

Tim Walter
Rhode Island College

Al Siebert
Oregon School of Education

Holt, Rinehart and Winston

New York   Chicago   San Francisco   Atlanta
Dallas   Montreal   Toronto   London   Sydney

Library of Congress Cataloging in Publication Data

Walter, Tim
  Student success.

  1. Study, Method of. 2. Success. I. Siebert,
Al, joint author. II. Title.
LB1049.W27   371.3'02812   76-1882
ISBN 0-03-015151-1

What Must This Book Achieve?

When we first talked about writing this book, we asked ourselves, "What must the student-success book achieve?" After much discussion we outlined three objectives:

1. It must give to each student who uses it a better chance of *success in school* than students who do not use it have.
2. It must show each student how to gain *better understanding* in each course and how to do so *more quickly*.
3. It must enhance self-development. That is, it must help each student to *take control* of his or her lifelong *self-education and personal development*.

Our next question, "How can these objectives be reached?" guided the development of this book. As you go through it, you will see that we try to focus your attention in two important directions.

The main focus is on practical tips about how to be more successful in school. We do more than just describe what to do, however. We also explain why these tips work. We explain useful principles of psychology that you can use on yourself.

The other focus is on how to be more successful as a person. We believe that *being successful as a student is part of being successful as an individual*. It is possible, of course, to be successful at passing courses without being successful in other areas of life and the reverse. In most instances, however, a student who is successful as a person is also successful in school.

Learning how to do well in school is part of having a good life. Both are important. And, contrary to what a few students seem to think, you don't have to choose between them. You can do both. Our view is that the best way to be successful in school is *not to study all the time*. By developing effective and efficient study skills, you can become a successful student and spend less time studying.

We believe that you should have time to engage in sports, be with friends, take naps, drive around, have dates, watch television, go hiking, or whatever you wish. That is why this book seeks to show you how to be more successful in school in a way that will give you more free time.

TIM WALKER
AL SIEBERT

How To Use This Book

First, skim through this book rapidly, and *ask yourself questions* about it. Go ahead and do that now. If you usually ask questions as you skim material, that is great! It means that you have an active mind and will grasp very quickly many of the principles that we present. If you have glanced through the book without asking questions, that is a clue: learning to ask questions is one of the first habits that you may want to work on.

Some questions that a person might ask while skimming through the book:

How can studying be easier?
Can I improve my intelligence?
What are some tips on how to pass exams better?
How can I write better papers more rapidly without having to write longer papers?
Why is there a whole chapter on goals?
What is the difference between being unsuccessful and not successful? Aren't the two the same?
What are successful people really like?
What kinds of games do losers play?
How can I have more good friends?

Second, don't think you have to do everything all at once! Pick several things that you believe are most likely to be quickly helpful, and try them first. Skip sections that you don't want to use yet.

This book is a compilation of many practical tips and psychological principles. It can take a long time to learn how to use them all. The key to the successful use of the book is not to try to do it all, at least not at the start. You'll burn yourself out. Try a few things until they become habits, and then work on building a few more habits.

Remember that habits take time to acquire. That is why this book could have been entitled *How To Become Successful Slowly*.

Contents

What Must This Book Achieve?   iii

How To Use This Book   v

1   HOW TO MAKE IT THROUGH SCHOOL   1

Develop Useful Habits   *2*
Choose Some Goals   *3*
Be Responsible for You   *3*
Use Psychology on Yourself   *4*

2   HOW TO MAKE STUDYING EASIER   5

Plan To Score   *6*
Set Up Your Schedule   *7*
Eliminate Distractions   *8*
  Visual Distractions   Auditory Distractions
  Territorial Distractions
Accept Your Humanness   *10*
  Concentration Span   Mandatory Breaks   Mix Study Subjects
Be an Active Learner   *13*
  The First Lecture   Take Lecture Notes
  Tips on Taking Notes   Active Reading
Write the Test   *14*
Checklist for Success   *15*

**3   HOW TO BECOME MORE INTELLIGENT AND SUCCESSFUL
IN YOUR CLASSES**   16

The Key to Studying and Becoming Intelligent   *18*
How To Ask Intelligent Questions   *18*
Generate Intelligent Questions   *19*
Reading = Question Answering   *20*
  *Increasing Your Reading Speed and Comprehension in
  Textbooks*

Reading Chapters in Textbooks   20
  Survey and Question   Read To Answer Questions
  Recite and Write Summaries and Answers   Review the Result
  Advantages of SQ4R   Difficulties of SQ4R
Predicting Exam Questions   24
Sources of Exam Questions   24
  Lecture Notes   Old Exams   Textbooks and Student Manuals
  Discussion Groups and Friends   Instructors   The Result
  How To Begin
Checklist for Success   30

4   DOING WELL ON TESTS AND PAPERS   **32**

Preparing for Tests   33
  Review and Test   Quiz Yourself   Making and Taking
  Practice Tests   Weekly and Final Practice Tests
  The Advantages of Preparation Strategies
Taking Your Instructors' Tests   36
  General Rules   Answering Objective Questions
  Answering Essay Questions   Answering Multiple-Choice
  Questions   Answering Matching Questions   Answering
  True-False Questions   Questions You Didn't Think You
  Could Answer   Write Comments about the Test
  Ask Questions During the Exam   The Advantages of These
  Test-Taking Strategies
Writing Papers for Instructors   40
  The Game Plan   Pick Your Topic   Ask Your Questions
  Write Your Answers   Arrange Your Answers   Rewrite Your
  Paper   Good Effort and Learning   Grammar, Spelling, and
  Neatness
Shape Up Your Instructor   44
  A Strategy for Teaching Your Teacher How To Teach
  One Final Tip
Checklist for Success   45

5   SETTING AND ACHIEVING YOUR STUDY GOALS   **46**

How To Set Goals   47
Scheduling Tasks To Achieve Goals   49
Steps in Scheduling   49
Uses of Recording Progress   49
  Keep Yourself on Schedule   Reduce Anxiety and Forgetfulness
  Record and Reward Your Progress
Developing Checklists   50
  Important Steps in Developing a Checklist   Benefits of
  Developing a Checklist   The Completed Checklist
Developing a Graph   56

Important Steps in Developing a Graph   Achievement and
Goal Lines   Benefits of Graphing
Rewarding Your Progress   58
The Importance of Rewards   Guidelines for the Use of Graphs,
Checklists, and Rewards

**6   CHARACTERISTICS OF SUCCESSFUL, UNSUCCESSFUL, AND
NOT SUCCESSFUL STUDENTS   59**

Self-Development Projects   60
Success in Reaching Your Goals   61
Behaviors   62
Time Management   64
Conduct Your Own Survey   65
Attitudes   65
Scoring Your Survey: How "Internal" Are You?   Positive and
Negative   SDP: Gaining a More Positive Attitude
Environments   71
Barbara's Plan for Changing Her Father   SDP: The Value of
Tracking Positives
Create Your Own Junta   75
Reference Groups   SDP: Discuss This Book
Learning Has Its Own Rewards   77
Checklist for Success   77
References and Suggested Reading   78

7   HOW TO BE A MORE SUCCESSFUL PERSON   79

Work Toward Self-Chosen Goals   81
Goals and Motivation   SDP: Questioning Your Career
Use Fantasies To Increase Your Motivation To Reach Goals   83
Four Fantasy Components Related to Motivation
SDP: Increase Your Achievement Motivation
Personality and Success   86
Actualize Yourself (But Take Care of Other Needs Too)   87
Developing Greater Self-Esteem   Self-Actualization
Beyond Self-Actualization   SDP: How To Be Self-Actualizing
Improve Your Self-Image   91
The Importance of Visualizing   SDP: Visualizing a Successful
You   Avoid Games Losers Play
Develop "Survivor" Traits   95
Observer   Loner   Crises   Self-Determined   Intuitive
Creative   Opposing Traits   Unique   SDP: Rate Your
Survivor Traits
Use a Practical Self-Development Plan   102
Checklist for Success   104

Is All This Really Necessary?   *104*
References and Suggested Readings   *105*

8   HOW TO HAVE A FEW GOOD FRIENDS   **107**

Have Frequent Contact   *109*
Be a Good Listener   *109*
  Accepting versus Judging   SDP: Guidelines for Starting
  Friendships
Goals in Friendships   *111*
  Manipulation   SDP: Guidelines for Successful Friendships

A CONVERSATION WITH THE AUTHORS   **114**

How To
Make It through School

DEVELOP USEFUL HABITS

You have heard talk about good study habits and poor study habits. What people are saying is that your *habits* determine whether or not you learn much during the time you spend in school. Two students may spend exactly the same amounts of time in classes and studying, but the student with good study habits learns more and gets a better education than the student with poor study habits.

When Benjamin Franklin was a young man, he discovered that habits are extremely important. In his autobiography he talks about how he decided to achieve moral perfection. He ran into difficulties, however. Here is how he describes his problem:

> I soon found I had undertaken a task of more difficulty than I had imagined. While my attention was taken up and care employed in guarding against one fault, I was often surprised by another. Habit took the advantage of inattention. Inclination was sometimes too strong for reason.

He analyzed the problem and eventually concluded

> that the mere speculative conviction that it was in our interest to be completely virtuous was not sufficient to prevent our slipping, and that the contrary habits must be broken and good ones acquired and established before we can have any dependence on a steady, uniform rectitude of conduct.

Franklin went on to describe the plan that he had worked out for acquiring the habits he knew were necessary. He would work on one habit at a time for one week at a time. He followed his plan for more than two years, checking himself daily to see how well he was doing in acquiring the habits he desired. He reasoned that, if he put constant mental effort into one desirable change for a week, the change should hold up during the next few weeks because of habit (see Chapter 7 for a fuller description of Franklin's self-improvement plan).

Students who want to improve have to work at acquiring habits they can count on. It isn't easy to develop new habits, but once you have them it makes life a lot easier. With good study habits you don't have to work so hard at studying.

CHOOSE SOME GOALS

When you were a child you were often asked, "What do you want to be when you grow up?" If you said "doctor," "airline pilot," "teacher," or something socially acceptable, then people were pleased. But what you told them was probably just part of a game you had to play.

The fact is that most students do not know what they want to be. They are waiting to see where life will take them and are curious about how things will turn out. When a student declares a certain area of study as his major it is often because the school requires him to declare something at registration time. This situation helps to explain why the motivation to study is low in some students. A goal that is forced on someone is not as motivating as a goal that is self-chosen.

The key to making it through school and learning something useful is to choose for yourself some goals that motivate *you*. Anything can be a goal. It may be to understand music, to learn about computers, to figure out how electricity works, to become a writer, to understand why economics is important to business and government, or to find out what causes nations to fight one another.

One way to choose motivating goals is to think ahead to the time when you will be out of school on your own. What knowledge, skill, or ability can you acquire that people will pay for? What would you enjoy doing that would be of value to others? What interests, hobbies, or talents do you have now that could be turned into a worthwhile occupation?

If you don't have any goals and can't think of any that make you feel excited about your future, you may see what your school's counseling center has to offer. There should be some interest and aptitude tests for you to take and some trained counselors to help you figure out what you would like to do with yourself.

BE RESPONSIBLE FOR YOU

Your success in school is your responsibility. It is not the responsibility of teachers, parents, friends, classmates, or administrators. Your teachers will present ideas and information, but whether or not you learn anything is mostly up to you.

3

Many students have been conditioned by magazines, television, and movies to be *passive*. They expect to be entertained by the textbook or the instructor. The only writings and speakers they pay attention to are those that capture and hold their attention. If an instructor teaches in a boring way, they are turned off. They seem to expect teachers to compete for their attention as professional entertainers do.

A student who feels responsible for getting something out of classes is *active*. He or she makes an effort to draw useful ideas from every instructor and is curious about what textbooks have to offer.

Remember that the best investment you will ever make is in yourself. You may lose your job or money, but no one can take your education away from you.

USE PSYCHOLOGY ON YOURSELF

Once you have chosen some goals for yourself and have accepted responsibility for your own learning, you've made a big step forward. You suddenly realize that you are in charge of your mind, your life, and your future. With this sense of responsibility comes the realization that you can start using psychology on yourself. You can purposefully use psychological principles of cause and effect to influence your own development and learning. For example, if you daydream in class and look around a lot, you can help yourself pay attention better by sitting in front—just as you would want to do at a concert or a football game. If you are a slow reader, you can take a reading-improvement course (most of them are free). If you waste a lot of time, you can begin associating with better students so that their habits will influence you. If you fall asleep easily, don't try to study sitting in a soft lounge chair or lying on the bed.

Psychologists have studied the principles of learning for many years. In the next chapter we outline many principles and conditions that you can use to improve how much you learn.

How To
Make Studying Easier

Studying is not the same as reading *Cosmopolitan* or *Playboy*, and reading a textbook is not the same as reading a novel. There can be a big difference between reading what interests you and reading an assignment. Most textbooks are not written to entertain you. You can't get away with reading only the parts that interest you. When it comes to studying, you must provide some of the motivation. Studying can be fun, but sometimes it is very hard work—as hard as physical labor.

Some students rely on will power to make themselves study. They grind away at their books week after week. But few can make it through the school year on will power alone. They run out of energy. They fall into a state of helplessness in which they may spend most of their time watching television or lying around. They feel bewildered. You hear statements like "I know I'm going to flunk if I don't study, but I can't even make myself open a book."

Once this condition develops, it is difficult to cure, so the best approach is to prevent it. And that is what this section is all about: how to study with less effort while learning more.

PLAN TO SCORE

Ernie walked into his counselor's office with a disgusted look on his face. So his grades were low! So what! He was the best sophomore halfback in the conference that year.

"Come in, Speedy."

Ernie smiled to himself. "Speed-E" was how the headlines read.

"Do you have any idea why I asked you to come in?"

"Grades?"

"Right, and it means you aren't getting much out of school."

"I try, but I don't have time."

"The coaches say you have been lifting weights and running with the cross-country team this spring, but that doesn't take more time than what other students are doing. You have the time. What are you doing with it?"

Ernie shrugged his shoulders.

"Your English grade is very low. When do you study English?"

"When I can."

"Tell me how the coach runs training camp."

Ernie brightened up. "He has this schedule every week. We do calesthenics, run wind sprints, pass and kick, learn plays, block and tackle, scrimmage. . . ."

"Right, and if you didn't train like that, could you win your football games?"

"No, you don't win if you're out of shape."

"Right. So if you are going to score in courses, what might you do?"

"Have a training camp?"

"Sort of. How about a weekly training schedule for yourself?"

Ernie looked out the window and nodded. Maybe this guy wasn't so dumb.

"Here's a blank schedule sheet. Take this pencil, and let's work out a weekly study schedule for you. Then you can put it up in your room just as the coach does with his schedule at training camp."

SET UP YOUR SCHEDULE

One of the greatest aids to any student is a study schedule. Start by purchasing a monthly calendar with spaces for you to fill in exam dates and dates when papers and projects are due. Marking exam times helps to keep you aware of what your studying is leading to. Next, fill in all the times that you plan to go to concerts, shows, or meetings; take trips; and so on. Now you are ready to make up a weekly schedule of your classes and the hours you plan to study. A weekly schedule gives you a clear picture of what you are doing with your time and helps you to spot an extra hour or two during the day that you can use for studying so that you can plan more free evenings to do what you want.

The steps for effective scheduling:

1. Establish a well-defined and reasonable schedule, one that you can live with.
2. Budget time to prepare for each class and all exams.
3. Study course notes as soon as possible after each class period, rather than waiting until a week before the exam.
4. Give difficult subjects preferred times with the fewest possible interruptions and disturbances.
5. Budget time for leisure activities and following through with them.

6. Stick to your schedule, and reward yourself for having achieved your study goals in the allotted time.

A schedule can have a motivating effect. Knowing that you have an hour on Thursday morning reserved for studying, you will be mentally prepared to spend that hour studying.

Warning: Do not allow yourself to study too much. Schedule time for the other things that you want to do, and stick to your schedule. Many students become so involved in their studying when they first start using the principles in this book that they keep right on studying through their scheduled breaks. Don't let yourself do this. When you reach the scheduled time to stop and go get some exercise, then do it! Make yourself stop studying!

The weekly schedule blank has been reproduced in Figure 1 so that you can make copies of it and post them in your room. But don't fill one out right now—we have more to say about study periods. First, we want you to look over your room.

ELIMINATE DISTRACTIONS

Visual Distractions

Beverly is like most students. She has created a comfy nest for herself in her room. It includes posters, ribbons, signs, photographs, letters, mugs with pencils, an old bottle, hats, high-school yearbooks, and several rocks. All these things have special meaning for her.

And that's the trouble. When she is studying, her mind is easily distracted from her textbook. The rock she sees from the corner of her eye reminds her of a weekend at the beach with a special person. The next thing she knows she has spent thirty minutes daydreaming.

If you study at your desk, you will be able to keep your mind on your studies more easily if your desk is free of mementos. Some students carry this principle too far, however. Some rooms look like monastic cells with nothing but bare walls and one small light on each desk. Although the bare walls make sense, the one small light does not. You may get more studying done, but your eyes may not last very long.

For minimum eyestrain your room should be well illuminated, with the main light source off to your side. A light directly behind or in front of you will be reflected from the glossy pages of your textbooks. This constant glare tires your eyes more quickly than indirect lighting. If you can't shift the lamp, shift your desk, placing it so that no portion of the bulb shines directly into your eyes. A strong light source pulls your eye toward it. The constant strain of trying to avoid looking at the light causes eye fatigue.

8

	Monday	Tuesday	Wednesday	Thursday	Friday	Saturday	Sunday
7–8							
8–9							
9–10							
10–11							
11–12							
12–1							
1–2							
2–3							
3–4							
4–5							
5–6							
6–7							
7–8							
8–9							
9–10							
10–11							
11–12							

Figure 1. Weekly schedule.

Auditory Distractions

"Quiet hours" rarely work as well as the rule makers hope. Distracting sounds still interrupt studying. Doors slam, phones ring, horns honk, planes fly over, and people move around. In fact, the quieter the study area, the more distracting these sounds become.

Steady background sounds "mask" distracting noises. One way to apply this knowledge is to play your radio or stereo softly while you study. Your purpose will be to create a steady background of "noise" to mask occasional sounds. Experiment with stations or records until you find what works best for you. F.M. radio stations playing instrumental music are usually best. Talk shows and fast-talking disk jockeys are usually worse for concentration than nothing at all. Some women say that turning on their hair dryers helps them to study, and one student reported that he tunes his radio to a place where there is no program—the static keeps him from being distracted.

Territorial Distractions

"Mary! Let's go over to the law library to study."

"Good idea, Ann! I might see that guy I met in the student union last week!"

Some students study in the library to escape from their rooms. It's a good idea, even when no library reading must be done, because the library atmosphere lends itself to studying.

Some students, however, use library time for combined advertising and scouting trips. The purpose is not to study but to find a date. There's nothing wrong with this notion, it's just that a student who goes to the library for this reason should not be surprised if little studying is done.

The problem is that, whenever we enter a new territory, our senses are drawn to the environment. We automatically scan new surroundings. We check the walls, floor, and ceiling. We look at the lights, decorations, and furnishings. We look at the people, wonder about certain sounds, and spend time adjusting to the feeling of a new chair. Every time you go to a new place you do the same thing. It is as automatic as the way a cat checks out new surroundings before it can settle down.

If you are serious about studying, pick one spot, and always study there. This will shorten your warm-up time, and allow you to concentrate on your studies better.

ACCEPT YOUR HUMANNESS

Concentration Span

Karen is a sophomore English major. During the summer she decided that when she came back to college she would study three hours every night without interruption. She put a sign on her door:

Off Limits from 7 to 10 P.M.
KEEP OUT
THIS MEANS *YOU*!

Is she getting lots of studying done? Yes and no. She has the ability to keep her body sitting at her desk for several hours at a time, but she has a problem that she hardly knows exists. While her eyes are looking at her book, her mind takes breaks. She sometimes finishes reading several pages and then realizes that she has no idea of what she has read. She has been daydreaming while reading!

Does Karen need more will power? No. She needs to accept the idea that she is a human being. She needs to accept the idea that there are certain limitations on what the human mind can be expected to do.

The way to make studying easy is to start with what you can do now and build on that. On the average, how long can you study before your mind slips off to something else? Forty-five minutes? Twenty-five minutes? Ten minutes? Most freshmen and sophomores find that they can concentrate on a textbook ten to fifteen minutes before starting to daydream.

Let's say that you find that your average concentration span is about twelve minutes. Now the question is *What would you like it to be*? Thirty minutes? Forty-five minutes?

Whatever goal you set for yourself, make certain you allow for your humanness. Be realistic. Set a goal that you can reach with reasonable effort, and give yourself enough time to reach it. As a rough guideline you might aim for a time span of fifteen minutes by the end of your freshman year, twenty-five minutes in your sophomore year, thirty-five minutes in your junior year, and forty-five minutes in your senior year. Graduate students should be able to study for about an hour without losing their concentration.

Mandatory Breaks

Once you have determined your concentration span, set up your study schedule so that you take a brief break after each study segment and a long break about once an hour. If you do, you will find that you can start and return to your studies much more easily than before.

In fact, you will find the end of a study segment coming so quickly that you will be tempted to continue. Don't do it. Keep your agreement with yourself. When you promise to take a quick break after twelve minutes, then do so. Do not allow yourself to study more than the allotted time.

A look at the records of most students shows why it is necessary to take these breaks even when you don't want to. With segmented study hours, studying is easier than expected. But after a while the old ways of studying creep back in.

What happens? The critical point comes when you reach the end of a study segment and find yourself so interested in the material that you decide to keep on. If you do, then your mind seems to say: "I can't trust you. You promised me a break after each fourteen minutes, but after I fulfilled my part you kept me working."

11

When you promise your mind a break after twelve or fourteen minutes, keep your word. No matter how much you want to keep on, make yourself take a short break. Get up and stretch. Walk out to get a drink of water or a breath of fresh air before starting the next study segment.

Mix Study Subjects

Mark is carrying a full load in school—English, biology, chemistry, psychology, and Spanish. He studies several evenings each week and uses that time for his toughest subjects. But, when he tries to recall what he's covered in an evening, he has trouble doing so.

Is Mark a slow learner? Probably not. The reason for his memory problem can be found in his study schedule. His evening study schedule looks like Figure 2.

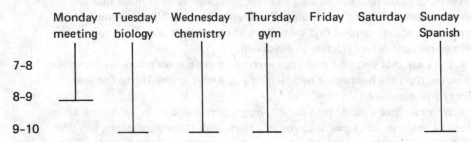

Figure 2. Mark's evening study schedule—before.

Mark's memory problem exists because he spends about three hours on one subject. When a person learns one set of facts and then goes on to learn a similar set of facts, the second set will interfere with his memory of the first, and the first will interfere with the second. The more similar material a person tries to learn at one time, the worse his memory will be.

How can you avoid this problem when you have lots of material to study? The best way is to mix your study hours with dissimilar material. Do not devote all of one evening to one subject. Switch subjects every hour or so, and always try to make your new subject as different as possible from what you have just finished. That way your mind can be assimilating one topic while you are reading about another. Mark did much better when he loosened up his schedule and initiated a study schedule like that in Figure 3.

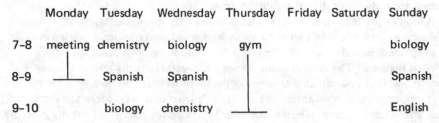

Figure 3. Mark's evening study schedule—after.

Although Mark's new schedule shows that he is mixing dissimilar subjects, he still may not be applying another principle of learning. Research shows that material learned by rote is retained better if immediately followed by sleep. Insightful learning can occur at any time and is not vulnerable to what follows immediately. This difference means that subjects like Spanish and chemistry tend to be remembered better if studied before bedtime.

BE AN ACTIVE LEARNER

The First Lecture

Successful students actively involve themselves in determining the requirements for each course. They then use their study time to engage in behavior most likely to help them achieve course success. During the first lecture find out from the instructor the answers to these key questions:

How will grading in the course be determined?
Which chapters in the textbook will be covered?
When will the exams be given?
What material will each exam cover?
What type of questions will be on the exams? Essay? Mutliple-choice?
What other work will be required?
When will it be due?
How will it be evaluated?
Does the instructor have an outline of the most important terms and concepts to be covered?
Should you read the chapter before the lecture each time?
What does the instructor hope each student will understand by the end of the course?

These questions are a starting point. Others will occur to you as you go along.

A word of caution: Don't make instructors feel that they are being cross-examined. Be assertive, but be *tactful*. If an instructor is not prepared to answer all these questions, back off. Try to find out when the information may be available. In general, you will find that instructors enjoy answering questions about what they believe is most valuable in their courses. A few are poorly prepared, however, and may become defensive if pressed too hard.

Some instructors will have the answers to most of these questions on written handouts. If you don't receive a handout, be sure to write everything down in a notebook.

Take Lecture Notes

By writing down what the instructor says in lectures you are helping yourself to be an active listener. You are also being realistic about the nature of human memory. Human beings quickly forget most of what they hear, no matter how much they would like to be able to remember.

13

Several days after hearing a lecture, the best that most students can do is to recall about 10 percent of what was said. So, unless you tape-record the lectures or alternate note taking with a friend, you need to take notes at every lecture.

Some students don't take notes. They may be trying an experiment to see whether or not they can get by without note taking, or they may have reasons for wanting everyone to know that they are not involved in the course. At any rate, if you ask a student who doesn't take notes to fill you in on something the instructor said last week, you will quickly learn for yourself how important note taking is for learning.

Tips on Taking Notes

Use large pages for taking notes. Don't put notes from more than one class on the same page. Put the date on each day's notes. Use an outline form as much as possible. Write down complete phrases and statements, rather than single words. Later on we'll give you more explicit tips about note taking.

Active Reading

Reading textbooks and lecture notes over and over again is an inefficient way to learn course material. Reading helps you to assess what you must learn, but it doesn't prepare you for doing well in tests, meeting course requirements, or developing understanding. Keep in mind that *if you are not studying as if you were preparing to take a test, you are wasting your time.*

WRITE THE TEST

"Hi, Speedy, how's it going?"
Ernie shook his head.
"What are you worried about?"
"I do the schedule, but they ask questions I don't know."
"The exams catch you by surprise. Right?"
Ernie nodded.
"How does the defensive unit prepare for a football game?"
"We run our offense the way the other team runs theirs. We study films and run their plays against our defense."
"Right. So how about doing that before exams?"
"Run plays?"
"Same thing. Get each instructor to tell you as much as possible about what the test will be like. Get copies of old tests to see what facts and ideas the instructor likes to emphasize. Each teacher has favorite points he likes to make, just as each team has favorite plays it likes to run. Find out if the questions will be multiple-choice, fill-in, or essay. Then pretend you are the instructor. Make up an exam just like the one he will give you. Or, better yet, get someone else in the class to give you a test like the instructor's."

Ernie looked away and nodded. "It might work. With one more good effort it might work." He looked back at the counselor for a moment and said, "Thanks." Then he grinned and headed off to his room.

CHECKLIST FOR SUCCESS

_____ Outline a weekly study schedule for yourself.

    _____ Avoid studying one subject too long. Change to a different subject every hour or so.

    _____ Schedule a brief period each day for reviewing lecture notes.

    _____ Don't schedule too much study time.

_____ Keep your study desk free of mementos.

_____ Play soft music to mask distracting sounds.

_____ Arrange good lighting.

_____ When you go to the library, try to study in the same place each time.

_____ Determine your concentration span, and set up study segments geared to your current span.

_____ Take short breaks after study segments and a long break each hour.

_____ Always study as if you were practicing to take tests.

How To Become More Intelligent and Successful in Your Classes

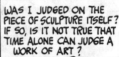

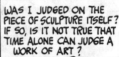

A "C"? I GOT A "C" ON MY COAT-HANGER SCULPTURE?

HOW COULD ANYONE GET A "C" IN COAT-HANGER SCULPTURE?

MAY I ASK A QUESTION?

WAS I JUDGED ON THE PIECE OF SCULPTURE ITSELF? IF SO, IS IT NOT TRUE THAT TIME ALONE CAN JUDGE A WORK OF ART?

OR WAS I JUDGED ON MY TALENT? IF SO, IS IT RIGHT THAT I BE JUDGED ON A PART OF LIFE OVER WHICH I HAVE NO CONTROL?

IF I WAS JUDGED ON MY EFFORT, THEN I WAS JUDGED UNFAIRLY, FOR I TRIED AS HARD AS I COULD!

WAS I JUDGED ON WHAT I HAD LEARNED ABOUT THIS PROJECT? IF SO, THEN WERE NOT YOU, MY TEACHER, ALSO BEING JUDGED ON YOUR ABILITY TO TRANSMIT YOUR KNOWLEDGE TO ME? ARE YOU WILLING TO SHARE MY "C"?

PERHAPS I WAS BEING JUDGED ON THE QUALITY OF THE COAT HANGER ITSELF OUT OF WHICH MY CREATION WAS MADE...NOW, IS THIS ALSO NOT UNFAIR?

AM I TO BE JUDGED BY THE QUALITY OF COAT HANGERS THAT ARE USED BY THE DRYCLEANING ESTABLISHMENT THAT RETURNS OUR GARMENTS? IS THAT NOT THE RESPONSIBILITY OF MY PARENTS? SHOULD THEY NOT SHARE MY "C"?

"THE SQUEAKY WHEEL GETS THE GREASE!"

Most of us believe that we are intelligent people, especially those of us in academic communities. A favorite pastime of many students and instructors who gather in classrooms, offices, coffeehouses, and dormitory rooms is to discuss that highly controversial subject "What is an intelligent person?" Is such a person creative? A wise decision maker? A person who thinks for himself? If we choose to go beyond these subjective definitions—all of which are certainly on target—we find one pre-dominant characteristic: An intelligent person can ask and answer important questions related to his or her field of interest.

If we lean back in our chairs and analyze what a successful student must do, it is clear that such a student must ask and answer intelligent questions. He must do so when writing papers, reading books, talking in discussion groups, making speeches, and, certainly, taking tests. Think of your textbook. It consists of a lot of answers to a lot of questions. Your professors and teaching fellows spend a good deal of time looking in textbooks to find questions to ask you in class or on tests. Think of the notes you take. Are they anything more than a set of answers to questions? Your instructors have carefully analyzed important books, speeches, films, and other documents to generate a body of information that they present to you in lectures. The final task for you is to answer important questions about things that you have been told in class, read in books, or watched in films.

Let's look at a simple and highly effective set of learning techniques that has been developed over the past fifteen years at The University of Michigan. Several thousand students who have used these techniques have found that, once they had learned to ask and answer intelligent questions, they became highly successful students, saved hundreds of hours in studying and preparing for courses, and were able to spend more time going to movies, watching television, chatting with friends, going on weekend trips, attending concerts, and generally leading the "good life."

If these things interest you, then let's spend a little more time discussing how you can learn the correct techniques. One thing we promise is that you will achieve your academic goals with a great deal more pleasure and far less pain then you have known in the past. We must sound one word of caution: This goal may require you to change many of your old habits. Such changes are sometimes difficult or painful. Why? Well, when you are used to a standard set of procedures to accomplish your goals, you often become comfortable with them and resist change. Even if you try the new techniques, you'll have a tendency to go back to the old behaviors. These old behaviors will help you to accomplish your goals to a degree but with the same pain and tremendous number of hours that you have spent in the past. Once you become accustomed to the new techniques, a lot of your old superstitious behavior related to studying and becoming educated will fade away. You will begin to get some good feedback from professors, friends, and yourself to indicate that the new methods save time. You will achieve your goals and have time to do things you never had time for in the past. Here we go!

THE KEY TO STUDYING AND BECOMING INTELLIGENT

Whenever you are reading from curiosity, allow your mind to go in any direction it wishes. But, when you study, *study as if you were practicing to take a test*. Practice answering questions! If you don't, you are wasting your time! Remember, it's your time, so why waste it?

HOW TO ASK INTELLIGENT QUESTIONS

What is an "intelligent" question?

It is first, one that you would like answered. Second, it is framed so that, in seeking the answer you will learn other things, that are important to you. Third, it is one that your instructor is likely to ask. Finally, it is a question that will help you to appear intelligent.

How do you learn to ask intelligent questions?

This question itself is a good one. Practice is the answer. Practice is a useful personal habit to acquire. At first it takes some work, but later the questions arise out of habit.

What will good questions help you to do?

They will help you to determine whether or not you and your instructor are interested in the same thing, to focus on the important points while listening and reading, to prepare for exams, to determine how ready you are to take an exam, to discriminate important from unimportant material, to determine the important points of lectures and readings, to influence your instructor, to save time.

What does a good question look like?

It usually starts with a phrase like

Give several examples of. . . .
Which of these is an example of. . . .
Describe the function of. . . .
What is significant about. . . .
List the important. . . .
Compare and contrast. . . .
Interpret the following. . . .
What is the structure of. . . .
Identify the following. . . .
Why does. . . .

GENERATE INTELLIGENT QUESTIONS

How can I determine what the important questions are?

Pretend that you are the instructor, and generate questions from your texts, lecture notes, and old exams. Think of questions before you go to class, and then listen to see whether or not other students ask the same questions or whether or not the instructor supplies answers to those questions.

Write out questions for a lecture or an assignment. Then, ask your instructor whether or not he thinks these questions are important and what other questions you should attempt to answer.

Do not be afraid to ask your instructor what he thinks are the important questions! Most instructors are happy to tell you what they think is important. Give them a chance, and they'll take a mile!

Ask your professor what goals he has for the students in his class. If you want a clear answer, you must learn to ask questions that help him to clarify for himself the questions he would like the class members to answer. You might ask

What should a student be able to do and what important questions should he be able to answer after having completed this chapter (unit, training, program)?
What important questions do you think we should be looking at in this unit (chapter, assignment)?
Can you suggest particular articles or books that highlight the issues we will be discussing in this unit?

19

What important things should we be looking for in this particular reading (film, case study)?

Such questions should be asked in as positive a manner as possible. Students have a tendency to put instructors on the defensive. It is your job to ask an instructor in what direction the course is headed and to reward him for telling you. A comment like "Thanks, that really clarifies things for me" is something an instructor responds to well and will increase the likelihood that you won't have to ask next time.

Now that I know what intelligent questions are and how they are determined, where do I begin?

We prefer to start by showing you how you can get a lot more out of your reading by turning it into a question-answering process. We'll then get into note taking, test taking, and a variety of other important study skills, but reading is the most important, so that's where we'll begin!

READING = QUESTION ANSWERING

Increasing Your Reading Speed and Comprehension in Textbooks

One of the fastest ways to spend less time reading assignments is to learn how to figure out the important questions and answers as quickly as possible. First, you should know that a large percentage (perhaps as many as 80 percent) of the words you read are redundant. Most words simply link ideas. The ideas are the answers to the questions you wish to answer.

Second, much of what you have to comprehend is already in your head. What you want are the answers to questions that you generate or find in the chapter as you survey and read.

Here are the steps you should go through to increase your reading speed and comprehension:

READING CHAPTERS IN TEXTBOOKS

Survey → Question → Read → Recite → Write → Review = the SQ4R Method

Remember, improved comprehension is the ability to answer more questions from reading assignments. This approach to reading is considered by many experts on study skills and reading improvement to be the most efficient and effective means for getting the most out of reading material in the least time. The primary concern of students using this method will be to *ask* and *answer* intelligent questions as they *read*.

What you should do is described in the following sections.

20

Survey and Question

The goal of surveying is to determine what important questions are answered in the textbook chapter. First, go to the end of the chaper to see whether or not there is a list of questions or a chapter summary. If so, read it right away! There is where you will find the important points that the authors wish to stress and the questions that students should be able to answer after completing the chapter.

If you can answer the questions and already know what is in the summary, you probably won't have to read the chapter. But don't decide that yet. If there is a set of questions or a chapter summary, you're ahead of the game; if not, you soon will be.

How do you survey? *The process of surveying involves quickly scanning the chapter to determine what important questions it answers.* Look for titles, subtitles, illustrations, pictures, charts, lead sentences in paragraphs, and questions that will give you a basic idea of what the chapter is about.

While surveying it is easy to turn titles, subtitles, and lead sentences into questions. For instance, "Communist Techniques of Brainwashing" is a paragraph heading in one psychology text. You have simply to turn it into "What were the techniques of brainwashing used by the Communists?"

By generating questions as you survey, you keep yourself alert to the important points in the chapter. Reading becomes an active, goal-oriented process. As you survey, you should formulate questions that, when answered, will give you a good summary of the chapter. *The result of your survey will be a list of questions.*

To prove your brilliance, you may wish to attempt to answer the questions you have generated in your survey before reading. This attempt serves to tell you how much you already know before spending an exorbitant amount of time reading. Many students are amazed at their ability to answer a large percentage of the questions they have formulated in their survey.

Another helpful technique is to summarize quickly what you already know about the chapter. By talking to yourself about the chapter, you help yourself to focus on the important questions you should be able to answer after having read it.

Read To Answer Questions

It is now time to read: Read as quickly as you can, in order to answer the questions you have generated while surveying the chapter and to find new questions and answers that you haven't predicted while surveying.

Remember: In many instances, your questions and answers will be summarized in titles, subtitles, or lead sentences. Occasionally, you may have to read beyond these headings for more important details. But not with the regularity that caused you to waste a lot of time in the past when you were looking for unimportant details.

When reading to answer questions, you learn to predict important questions before spending a lot of time reading. You learn to read selectively. You read to find answers to questions. When you come to the answer to a question that you hadn't predicted, you simply slow down, formulate the question, and make sure you know the answer. When you come to material you already know, you keep on going to find out what you don't know.

Recite and Write Summaries and Answers

Now that you have read to answer the questions from your survey and have developed new questions and answers that you hadn't predicted, it is important to go one step farther.

Recite or write a short summary of what you have just read. This procedure is an excellent way of proving to yourself that you have asked and answered the important questions from each chapter.

You should practice talking to yourself (even if people think you're a little crazy) about the answers to your questions. Most people wish to rush on to a new chapter before thoroughly proving to themselves that they are familiar with the contents of the last. They say to themselves: "I read it. I know what it's about."

Equally important, recite and write the answers to the questions that you developed while surveying and reading. This procedure will help you to prove to yourself that you really comprehend the chapter.

Review

If you have followed the steps so far, you are in excellent shape to review the chapter at any time. You will have a set of questions and answers representing the contents of the chapter. When preparing for your exam, quiz yourself on these questions until you feel comfortable that you could give very accurate answers to them if they were to appear on your exam.

We also suggest summarizing to yourself, orally or in writing, the contents of the chapter and comparing your summary with the one you wrote after having read the chapter.

Taken together, these activities will really give you the feeling that you've mastered the material. When you know you can answer questions correctly and make accurate summaries, you will be more confident that you have mastered the chapter. You will spend less time attempting to reread chapters and involve yourself less in a variety of superstitious and time-consuming study activities that seldom help you to ask and answer important questions.

The Result

You have now

1. Surveyed the chapter
2. Generated questions
3. Read selectively to answer the questions in greater detail
4. Found questions and answers that you hadn't predicted

5. Recited and written answers to questions and chapter summaries
6. Reviewed the chapter by practicing answering questions and summarizing the chapter.

You should now have a good understanding of the chapter.

Why should I believe that this approach works?

Evidence collected at The University of Michigan Reading Improvement Service and other learning centers has shown that most good readers use these techniques. Students who use them improve their grades, reduce their study time significantly, and increase their reading speed and comprehension of the textbook.

Advantages of SQ4R

You spend less time memorizing facts that you will soon forget.

You don't waste time reading and looking for things you already know.

Your preparation for tests is a continual process. By the time you take the test you will find that you have answered most of the questions.

You focus on grasping the key concepts. Details are then much easier to remember.

You don't waste time looking for details that are unimportant to you or your instructor.

You learn to take an expert's point of view and to think things out for yourself.

You learn to sit down and generate answers that you didn't think you knew. You then search for additional information, which makes polished answers out of incomplete ones.

You learn to organize and structure your studying. You state your goals as questions, seek answers, achieve your goals, and move on.

Difficulties of SQ4R

It is difficult to change old study patterns. You may be accustomed to reading every word, always afraid that you're going to miss something. Such a new technique may appear reckless and inappropriate to learning. It takes more energy to ask questions and generate summaries than it does passively to let your eyes read printed pages. It is easier just to open a book and start reading.

How can you reconcile these points? There are advantages and disadvantages to *everything*! This is true both for being a successful student and for being a poor student. If there were no disadvantages, if it were easy, then everyone would be more successful. There are costs, but, once you are into SQ4R, the gains are worthwhile.

Try the techniques, and look for results like the following:

The quality of your questions and answers will improve with practice.

The amount of time it takes you to generate questions and summaries will decrease.

The amount of time it takes to verify and improve your answers will decrease with practice.

You will be able to cover large amounts of material in far less time.

You will find that you are producing the same questions as your instructors, textbooks, and friends.

With practice, you will find that the summaries you generate come closer to those of the author.

These techniques are based on several well-established learning principles. First, when you learn material under conditions that are similar to those under which you will be tested, there is a greater likelihood that you will remember it. People learn meaningful material faster than they memorize unrelated or nonsense information. Learning new material is easier when you associate it with familiar material.

The SQ4R Method sounds helpful, but could I start by just using parts of the technique or using the whole technique on small sections of my work?

Our students report best results when they begin practicing the entire technique at once. But some people will adjust best to the SQ4R strategy by practicing on a small section of work to see immediate results. They gradually increase the use of this method as they become more comfortable with it.

PREDICTING EXAM QUESTIONS

How do I go about predicting exam questions from sources other than my text?

Once you accept the value of always studying as if you were practicing to take a test, you'll be on the right track. It is important to gear your study behavior collection of questions and answers that you expect to find on your exams. By using the reading techniques that we have suggested, you will have a good start. Your reading will always be geared to asking and answering important questions.

In addition to this style of reading, there are several other techniques that will help you to collect a good set of exam questions. Note taking, asking friends and instructors, collecting old exams, holding discussion groups, and using textbook and student-guide questions are several that we suggest. Let's start with note taking.

SOURCES OF EXAM QUESTIONS

Lecture Notes

Think of your lectures as textbook chapters. Each usually has a main theme and makes several important points. If you listen for them, they will be easier to hear.

We encourage you to take lecture notes in outline form. This habit will help you to focus on the main points that can be turned into questions. Your job is to record these questions and to make sure that you know how your instructor would answer them.

Most good instructors answer their questions thoroughly in class, but sometimes they only allude to the answers. Wise students always make sure they know what questions the instructor believes are important. They then go to outside sources if more information is needed than has been supplied in the lecture.

Here are the steps we suggest that you follow in taking lecture notes:

1. During the lecture, take notes on the right-hand side of the paper. Leave a large margin on the left.
2. After the lecture, take several minutes to turn your outline into test questions. The main theme and subtopics can be turned into questions. Usually each lecture will supply you with three to seven good exam questions. They should be written in the left-hand margin.
3. At least once a week, review the questions you have asked. Pretend that you are taking a test. Give yourself an oral quiz, or, even better, practice by taking a written quiz. Then compare your answers to those given in your notes or textbook.

Remember: This procedure will help to make something meaningful out of lectures that often leave you in a quandary. Your purpose is to go to lectures looking for questions and their answers. If you come out of each lecture with several questions and answers, you'll be pleased. They're likely to be on your next test!

Your notes may not look as neat as those in Figure 4, but we don't expect you to carry a typewriter to class. If your notes are neat and as close to outlined as possible, you'll have a much better chance of turning them into a good set of questions. Those in Figure 4 were taken at an introductory psychology lecture. The topic was hypnosis, and the notes represent a portion of the total lecture.

Old Exams

Students often feel guilty when they admit to having looked over past exams. They feel that they have been cheating. Our answer to this is "bunk!" Looking at old exams tells you what an instructor thinks is important information for which students should be responsible.

Looking at old exams doesn't guarantee that you'll know exactly what your exam questions will be. Instructors change their lectures, textbooks, films, guest speakers, and even their own opinions once in a while. Consequently, exams change from semester to semester.

Nevertheless, by looking at old exams you may answer several important questions:

1. Does the instructor have some favorite questions that he asks every year?
2. Do test questions appear to be taken from material similar to that which you are studying?

Questions	Notes
	Anton Mesmer
	1. Cures by magnetism—capture magnetic fluids from planets to cure sickness
	2. Put magnets over patients to cure them
	3. Cures due to placebo effect—power of suggestion
How did Mesmer bring about the "grand crisis" in his patients and what was the effect?	4. Mesmer's Grand Crisis a. Mesmer dressed in robes like wizard b. Patients in tubs of magnetized water c. Patients went into trance-like states d. Mesmer had discovered hypnosis e. Mesmer urged patients to go into "grand crisis"—like convulsive seizure
What are some of the reasons people gave for the the effects of Mesmerism?	f. Mesmer convinced that "grand crisis" was responsible for cures of patients g. Mesmerism was name given to technique for inducing trance state and the "grand crisis"
Why was Mesmerism banned in Paris?	h. French government investigated Mesmerism and said it was a hoax—cures due to suggestion and imagination rather than magnetism i. Mesmerism was banned from France on moral as well as medical grounds and Mesmer retired to town outside Paris
	Hypnosis
	1. Name is taken from Greek word for sleep
Why did Charcot believe some patients could be hypnotized more easily than others?	2. Jean Charcot said there was a close connection between hysteria and hypnosis and that only hysterics could be hypnotized
	3. French scientists rejected Charcot's claim and insisted that hypnosis was a result of suggestibility
What effect did studying hypnosis have on Freud's view of mental illness?	4. Freud and hypnosis a. Studied under Charcot—after his studies he began to think of mental illness as being due to psychological rather than physiological causes b. Freud used hypnosis to suggest to patients that their symptoms could disappear—this worked sometimes, but they often recurred c. Freud found that only patients who experienced a strong personal trust in him could be easily hypnotized d. Freud renounced hypnosis as a therapeutic tool and developed the technique of free association

Figure 4. Sample lecture notes.

3. Do test questions come primarily from lecture notes, readings, or from a variety of sources?
4. What types of questions does the instructor prefer: multiple-choice, short-answer, true-false, essay?
5. On which content areas does the instructor place the most emphasis?
6. Should you be asking and answering questions about particular areas that the instructor views as more important than you would have predicted?
7. Does the instructor expect students to give detailed explanations or is he simply interested in students' understanding of basic concepts?

These questions should help you see the value of reading and taking notes in the question-answer format. There is no guarantee that the instructor will take most of the questions from the same source that he used in years past. Yet it is surprising how similar questions are from year to year regardless of the textbooks that instructors use. They often choose new textbooks that give better answers to the same questions that they have been asking for many years. Equally important, few instructors make drastic changes in their course notes from semester to semester. They usually only up-date them. The questions you generate from course notes, textbooks, and other sources, combined with old exam questions, will thus be invaluable in your exam preparation.

Textbooks and Student Manuals

In addition to gathering questions and answers from reading assignments, you should find that textbooks and student manuals offer a wealth of information. Always check each chapter to determine whether or not a set of questions precedes or follows the chapter. Such questions are included by authors for one reason: They believe that students should be able to answer them after having read the chapter.

Many instructors take their test questions directly from those in the textbook. Surprisingly, many students never look at these questions. They seem to feel that no one could be so stupid as to tell them exactly what they should be able to do after reading the chapter.

Authors usually try to help students, not to trick them! If you are not in the habit of answering chapter questions, we recommend them as the starting point in your effort to organize a good set of questions and answers.

Just as important are the student manuals that accompany many introductory textbooks. They have been designed to inform you of the study behaviors that will be helpful to students using the textbooks. Student manuals often contain true-false, multiple-choice, fill-in, and short essay questions. Even if your exam is likely to be made up of questions that differ in style from those found in the student manual, the manual questions are still valuable. You have only to change them into the style likely to be found on your next test. This approach is far easier than avoiding the manuals because they are in a programmed format that may turn you off. Student manuals are designed to save you time; use them to your advantage. You may find that by using them you save enough time to watch a little extra television.

Discussion Groups and Friends

Some of the most important sources of test questions, yet often the most over-looked, are friends and fellow students. By talking with other students enrolled in the course or with students who have been enrolled in past semesters, you can formulate an excellent perspective of the types of questions and answers you should be looking for. Just as important is finding out what you might avoid.

Many students believe it's difficult to organize formal study groups. Some simply have a preference for working on their own. This strategy can be self-defeating. By organizing the questions and answers you have derived from a variety of sources, you are in an excellent position to compare yours with those of fellow students.

We compare this process with the old pastime of trading cards. You collect as many as you can and simply trade off your extras to build up an even stronger set. Similarly, you find out what questions other students feel are important. You compare your answers to theirs, to ensure that you haven't overlooked important information. Everyone comes out stronger than when he entered the game. Everyone is better prepared to ask and answer intelligent questions.

After organizing a group of several (three or four) students who are taking the same course, you should all agree on a standard meeting time. The group's goal during the meeting is to have each member offer a series of questions and answers likely to be on the next exam. Group members should look over one another's questions and answers. You may wish to quiz one another on specific points that you believe are important. This process facilitates learning, saves time, perfects your answers, and provides group members with feedback indicating that they are on the right track.

After compiling the questions and answers of group members, you will have a good model of your next test. Your job is to practice asking and answering the questions to ensure that you will be prepared for the exam. The group can then meet after each test to determine how accurately its members have been able to predict the questions and answers on the exam.

The truth of the old adage "Two heads are better than one" is really brought home when you see how well a group of three or four students is able to predict what information is important to comprehend for a given subject.

Should you not care to work with a group, our alternative recommendation is that you find one friend or classmate with whom you can exchange practice exams. You may find it easier to form a "study group" with just one other person—possibly your girlfriend or boyfriend, which should surely add an incentive. The collection and exchange of questions and answers are the basis of this technique. You will find it helpful to make up practice tests for each other. By quizzing and talking to each other, you will refine your answers and convince yourself of the value of this exercise.

By studying in a group or with one other person, you will help to ensure that you

1. Structure a situation in which other people will encourage you to involve yourself in the study activities we have recommended
2. Ask and answer questions that you believe are important and are likely to be found on your next exam
3. Share your questions and answers with others
4. Find questions that you yourself hadn't predicted
5. Refine your answers with additional information supplied by other students
6. Put together practice tests
7. Take practice tests under conditions that closely resemble those under which you will be tested
8. Evaluate the results of the suggested procedure by comparing your practice tests with those given by the instructor
9. Develop a most efficient and effective process of preparing for exams.

Instructors

At the risk of sounding bold, we suggest that your instructor is the best source of information on forthcoming test questions. Many students find it difficult to ask instructors what they believe is important. As we suggested earlier, most instructors are happy to tell you what they think is important. Give them a chance: Ask them!

Throughout the semester it is your job to ask the instructor what is important, what questions you should be able to answer. When it comes time to take the exam, you must narrow things down even farther. You should find out specifically what will be covered on the exam and the structure of the questions: Will they be short-answer, multiple-choice, or whatever?

Ask your instructor: "Could you specify the areas in which we should concentrate our studying?" "Are there particular issues which you feel we should devote more time to than others?" "Are there specific questions which we should look at as a guide to studying the most important issues?"

Remember, be pleasant to instructors when asking such questions. Don't pick at them! Treat them as scholars whom you are trying to imitate. Show interest in their courses, and ask questions in as sincere a manner as possible. Whatever you do, don't ask: "Are there any areas you feel are unimportant?" "Which of these chapters should we avoid, considering all that we have to study for this test?"

If you ask such questions the instructors may be so peeved that they will assign the encyclopedia. Most instructors believe that everything they teach is important and that you should agree. In trying to determine what is likely to be on exams, your goal is simply to persuade instructors to narrow down all the important things they have told you to a precise statement of what your exam will look like. If you are pleasant and thank your instructors for their help, you'll be way ahead of the game. You may even find out the exact format of the exam and which questions are most important!

The Result

Predicting exam questions is the most useful technique we have found in preparing students to learn the important concepts covered in their courses. Equally important, it helps them to pass their exams with much greater ease. If you have followed our suggestions, you will have collected exam questions from

1. Your textbook chapters
2. Your lecture notes
3. Old exams
4. Lists of questions in your textbooks
5. Lists of questions in student manuals
6. Discussion groups and friends
7. Your instructor.

Once you have collected a good set of test questions, you will be better prepared to follow through with the procedures we shall suggest in Chapter 4, on tests.

Is the purpose of education to learn how to answer instructors' questions and pass tests?

Yes and no! If you want to understand the experts and even go beyond them, it is important to be able to ask and answer the same questions that they believe are important. If you're realistic, you know you have to pass the requirements of the course. If you understand what your instructors wants, then you will learn a lot. If your instructor is less than adequate, then it is a matter of meeting his criteria and going on to better courses. There is no need to waste a lot of time in the process.

How To Begin?

It is best to begin by practicing predicting and answering exam questions!

Each week, count those questions and answers that you have collected from textbook chapters, old exams, lecture notes, student manuals, discussion groups, classmates, and your instructors. To monitor how well you are doing, graph the number of questions and answers you have for each class (see Figure 5).

CHECKLIST FOR SUCCESS

Here is a list of guidelines that will help you to monitor your studying and your success at implementing the learning strategies described.

____ Practice reading to answer questions.

____ Practice writing chapter summaries.

____ Generate questions from lectures, textbooks, chapter summaries, student manuals, old tests, and discussion groups.

____ Ask your instructor what goals he or she has for the students in class.

____ Keep a weekly record of the numbers of questions and answers you generate for each class.

Questions

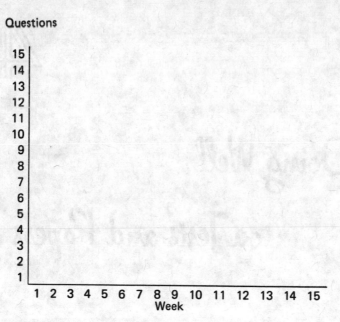

Figure 5. Graph for predicted exam questions.

4

Doing Well

on Tests and Papers

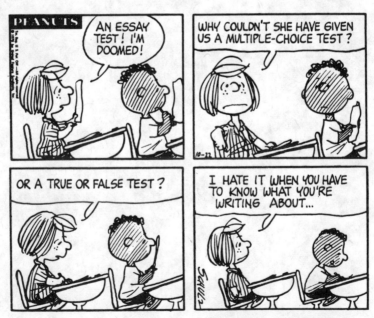

© 1970 United Feature Syndicate, Inc.

PREPARING FOR TESTS

Now that I have collected a good set of questions and answers, how can I make sure that I'll do well on the tests?

Periodically, go through the questions you have generated to see whether or not you can still answer them. Avoid saying to yourself, "I know the answer to that one." Verbalize or write the answer to prove to yourself how brilliant you have become!

Review and Test

Using the questions you have collected, make up practice tests. Take them under conditions as close as possible to actual test conditions. Then compare your answers with those you have generated from your textbooks, lectures, and so on.

Quiz Yourself

Here are some specific hints about making and taking practice tests, strategies for taking tests, and other useful preparation techniques.

Many students find it helpful to write their questions and answers on 4 x 6-inch cards. As you collect questions from the sources we have suggested, transfer them to the cards. The answers should be placed on the backs of the cards.

This system is similar to the old flash-card system that many of us have used in learning our multiplication tables, spelling, and foreign languages. Most students like this system because it gives them a central filing system of questions and answers. Rather than fumbling through review of notes and textbooks, they go to their stacks of question cards and quiz themselves.

That sounds great for most students, but what about those of us who spend most of our time working problems in math and science? How can this technique help us?

One of the most important insights that students can develop is recognition that success in a particular course is based upon solving specific problems, especially in mathematics, chemistry, physics, and engineering.

Review for students in these courses should be no different from review for other students. They must practice working problems as similar as possible to those that will be found on their next exam. By recording sample problems on 4 x 6-inch cards, they will develop files of important problems that they should be able to solve if they wish to advance to more complex mathematical and scientific problem solving.

How about students in foreign languages? Should they review in the same way?

Yes, all students should review by practicing answering the important questions that are likely to appear on their next tests. Language students must maintain basic vocabulary and grammatical skills if they wish to develop more complex language skills. By reviewing these areas, they assure themselves of continued involvement in the basics upon which more complex skills are built.

Making and Taking Practice Tests

Practicing the exact behavior you will be required to perform in a test situation not only prepares you to do well; it also helps you to relax and builds your confidence. After successfully passing practice tests, students seldom feel the uneasiness and tension that have accompanied old study routines. They know they have studied the right questions, and they sleep better for knowing. Here is how to make and take practice tests.

1. Determine the amount of time you'll be given to take your instructor's exam; take practice tests over the same length of time. Taking them under realistic time pressure is important. If you force yourself to do so, you'll feel more comfortable when you're actually in the testing situation.
2. Arrange the questions you've been accumulating from chapters, lecture notes, study groups, old exams, and so on into practice tests.
3. Try to put the questions into the same format that the test will offer (multiple-choice, short essay, and so on). Old tests will give you a good idea of the format your instructor is likely to use.

4. Take your practice tests under conditions as similar as possible to those under which you'll be tested. The classroom in which you'll be tested is the best place to take practice tests. If it is not available to you, make sure you practice in a room in which you won't be bothered.
5. Try to answer your questions without referring to your books or other sources of information.
6. When attempting to answer questions for which you need more information, try to guess and make up things as if you were in a real testing situation and trying to earn at least partial credit. This procedure forces you to take what you already know and to determine what might be the answer, rather than saying, "I just don't know!" Yes, this approach is known as "bulling," and it often makes the difference between an A and a B! Bulling is writing out an answer that makes sense to you, even though you don't remember exactly what was said in the textbook or lecture. It requires the use of your imagination.
7. Once you have completed the test, compare your answers with those that you have in your own set of questions and answers. Use your textbooks and notes to refine your answers.
8. After noting the questions you have answered well and those in need of improvement, design a new test. Follow the same procedure that we have outlined in steps 1–7. Take the new test and continue repeating the steps until you think you have mastered all the questions and answers likely to appear on your instructor's test.

Weekly and Final Practice Tests

When you take weekly practice tests in each subject area, you'll find that exam panic and last-minute cramming are a thing of the past. Before each scheduled test, take a comprehensive practice test made up of sample questions from your weekly tests. You'll be pleasantly surprised at how much easier it is to pass your final practice test when you have been taking weekly tests.

This process allows you to master smaller amounts of information each week and then to put everything together in a final practice test just before you take the real thing.

The Advantages of Preparation Strategies

But isn't this strategy very time consuming?

It may appear so, but we have found that students who concentrate on collecting test questions and answers, taking weekly practice tests (or quizzes), and taking final practice tests spend far less time on irrelevant and wasteful studying. They practice exactly what their instructors will require of them, "asking and answering intelligent questions."

TAKING YOUR INSTRUCTORS' TESTS

Now that you know how to prepare for a test, let's make sure that you know how to relax and use your time wisely once you have the real test in your hands.

General Rules

1. Read the instructions to determine the types of questions you'll be expected to answer. Determine where you'll earn the most points. Don't spend a lot of time reading; just form a basic idea of how the test is set up, and plan your attack.
2. Divide your time to ensure that you schedule enough for all portions of the test. Otherwise, you'll devote too much time to the most difficult parts and wind up "choking" when you find that you won't be able to complete the whole test.
3. Before starting, determine whether or not answering the easier questions will earn you just as many points as answering the more difficult questions. If so, complete the easy ones first. After answering them you'll have more confidence, and you will be able to pass on to the more difficult questions.
4. Make sure you understand what each question is asking. If the directions say, "Give several examples of . . . ," then do exactly that! Give instructors exactly what they ask for.
5. If you don't understand a question or find it extremely difficult, place an X by it, and move on to easier questions. You can come back later. This procedure saves time and prevents anxiety. Most important, you may find the answer hidden in other questions as you move through the test. Don't waste precious time trying to dig it out from the back of your brain.

Answering Objective Questions

Never, never leave an answer blank, unless there is a penalty for guessing. If there is a penalty, guess only when you can eliminate at least half the possible options, two options when there are four in a multiple-choice question, for example.

Read objective questions carefully, but answer them quickly. Don't change an answer later unless you are *sure* that your new answer is correct. Your first answer is more likely to be correct. Analyses of students' answer sheets show that, if you start changing answers, you're more likely to hurt than to help your score.

Write legibly! You'll pick up extra points from instructors for precision and other virtues. Actually, they just like the neat appearance of your papers.

Answering Essay Questions

Outline your answer to an essay question before writing it. In this way you will ensure that you include key ideas for which you will earn points from the grader.

The procedure saves time in the long run. You can organize your answer and can be sure to include everything that is important. You will feel more organized when you begin to write and will have fewer uncertainties about whether or not you have included everything that you should.

DEFINE TERMS

Define the terms that you will use in your answer. Be sure to call attention to any uncertainties in your mind about the question asked. This approach often clarifies for the instructor why you have answered the question in a particular manner.

USE SUBHEADINGS AND EXAMPLES

As you write, be sure to use subheadings for longer answers. They help the reader, and you yourself feel some organization in your answer. It is crucial to use examples to support your main points. There is less opportunity to argue about whether or not you really know what you are talking about if you can present several examples to substantiate your position.

POLISH ANSWERS

Above all, write legibly! After you have finished writing, pretend that you are the grader. Ask yourself: "Have I misread or misinterpreted the questions? What did I leave out? Have I made any careless mistakes?" Allot time at the end to polish your answers, add necessary points, and deal with more difficult questions that have puzzled you.

Answering Multiple-Choice Questions

As you answer multiple-choice questions, always be sure to eliminate the obviously incorrect answers first. You will save considerable time and will help to reduce any anxiety about choosing the correct answer.

Read and answer each question quickly. After you have answered all questions, go back, and check to see that you have read them correctly. If you have time, reread them all. If not, reread those that you marked with X the first time through because you were unsure of your answers. Never change an answer when rereading unless you are absolutely certain your new answer is correct.

Answering Matching Questions

Check to make sure you have read the directions for matching questions carefully. Sometimes students believe that matches are so obvious that they do exactly the opposite of what is asked. If the instructions say, "Match those that are different" or "Match those that are opposite," you'll feel rather foolish if you have spent a lot of time matching those that are similar.

A real time saver is answering the easy ones first. This tactic reduces the chance of guessing incorrectly on more difficult matches.

Answering True-False Questions

Never waste a lot of time pondering true-false questions. Many students have been known to waste major portions of test periods attempting to "solve" true-false questions as if they were Chinese puzzles. If an answer isn't immediately apparent, don't become frustrated. Simply move on to the next question. Just one or two questions aren't worth that many points. They don't deserve the precious time that could be devoted to other, more important questions. The points you miss on a true-false question can usually be picked up later in an essay question through some rather shrewd use of your imagination, which we have called "bulling."

A classic mistake of students is to come back later and to change a number of true-false answers. Avoid this mistake at all costs. As we mentioned, your first answer is likely to be correct. If you start changing them, you'll usually be worse off than if you left the original answers.

Questions You Didn't Think You Could Answer

Students are often amazed when we ask them to try answering questions and writing summaries after simply surveying a chapter. They say, "But I haven't read it yet!" They then go ahead, do it, and find that their answers and summaries are fairly accurate, sometimes close to perfect. How do they do it? Stored in their brains they have so much information of which they are unaware. When they force themselves to start talking about what they know, they're often amazed.

We want you to remain humble, but on the same note we want you to be able to pull yourself out of jams by answering questions to which you don't have immediate answers. In a test situation only you can answer the question (unless you wish to risk the chance of being thrown out for cheating).

What can you do when you come to a question that baffles you? Try to remember that in your reading you're likely to have picked up some information that is relevant. If that's all you write, you're likely to earn a few points, which is more than you'll have if you leave it blank. While taking the exam, you're likely to pick up some information related to the answer you need. If you can't figure out the exact answer, you can probably figure out an approximation, especially in math, in which students may often work out problems and come up with incorrect answers. They may not receive complete credit, but partial credit is surely better than a big zero.

Using your imagination takes practice and even a little confidence. It is not the most important study skill that we can recommend, but it can be valuable at times.

You Can Write Comments about the Test

If, in spite of all your excellent preparation, you are still quite nervous about the test then try imagining that written across the top of the test is the statement, "Feel free to write comments about the test items."

Wilbert J. McKeachie, known for his research on ways to improve teaching, discovered that, when this statement was printed at the top of tests, many students did better. The students who were helped most were those who had stronger than average fears of failing. And an interesting result was that it didn't matter whether they actually wrote anything about the test or not! Just the presence of the statement was enough to improve the scores of students who had strong fears of failing.

So, when you are taking a test, remember that you should *feel free to write comments about the test items*! If you believe that a question is poorly worded, then say so. But *also* go on to explain why and perhaps to suggest a better wording. The whole purpose of the examination is to show that you know something about the subject. *Note:* If you have doubts about the instructor's allowing comments on the questions, then go ask!

Ask Questions During the Exam

Instructors know that their questions are not always clear. Sometimes the wording isn't as good as it should be. That's why most instructors will answer questions about test questions during exams.

Take advantage of this willingness. If there are one or two questions that just don't compute, go ask the instructor such questions as "When was this material covered?" "I saw all the films but don't remember the one that this was covered in; can you give me any clues?" "Where was this information presented in the textbook?" "The way this item is worded, there are several possible answers, this one and this one. Which do you want?"

If you are drawing a blank anyway, you have nothing to lose by seeing whether or not the instructor will give you some hints. He will not give you the answer, but a comment like "That item is from the chart at the end of Chapter 7" may give you the clue you need. Try it. Asking the instructor for clues can be worth several extra points on every exam.

The Advantages of These Test-Taking Strategies

Purely and simply, the strategies described in this chapter can improve your confidence by encouraging you to attack your tests in a reasonable and predictable manner. By using these techniques, you should achieve more points on any given test.

When taking tests, you will find that you don't make those stupid mistakes that make you want to kick yourself and ask, "Why didn't I use my brain?" You will read the questions carefully, plan your time well, determine the value of specific questions, and answer them in ways likely to earn the maximum number of points. You will engage in test-taking behaviors that we most often observe in students who comprehend their course material and do well on exams. In essence, you will be a more successful student and will still have time for friends!

Again we emphasize that students who use these techniques *seldom*

1. Misread the test questions and answer them incorrectly
2. Waste time on questions that stump them

3. Waste time answering questions with information they know is irrelevant
4. Run out of time and fail to complete the test
5. Lose points as a consequence of changing their answers at the last minute
6. Have difficulty answering questions that require them to "bull" a little
7. Develop exam panic when a test appears more difficult than they had predicted
8. Fail tests (they usually receive B or better).

Students who use these techniques report that they

1. Seldom (and we mean *seldom*) "choke" in exams
2. Get better grades on tests
3. Receive more points for answers than they would have predicted
4. Feel more relaxed and confident while taking tests
5. Feel confident that they haven't wasted their time while answering complex as well as simple questions
6. Feel better organized while taking tests
7. Seldom leave out important information from answers
8. Are able to complete exams in the allotted time.

WRITING PAPERS FOR INSTRUCTORS

The Game Plan

The successful way to write papers closely parallels the steps you take in preparing for and taking tests. Again books and lectures should be viewed as sets of answers to questions. It is the student's job to read textbooks and to take lecture notes in such a way that he can determine the important questions and answers that instructors would like him to comprehend. We carry this approach one step farther and encourage students to ask the following question when writing a paper for an instructor: "What important questions should I answer in this paper?"

For students willing to approach writing from this perspective, we have found the process to be less difficult and time-consuming. Most important, their papers are precise, accurate, and well received by instructors. Here are the steps we suggest for planning and preparing papers.

Pick Your Topic

Pick the topic you find most interesting! Try to make it a topic that your instructor believes is important. By listening closely in class you will often detect certain interest areas that are the instructor's favorites. Our students have found it best to choose topics that they and their instructors have enjoyed doing research on and reading about.

Instructors tend to supply bibliographies and other information about their favorite subjects. It may be helpful to talk with them after class or to make appointments to discuss your papers. Talking with them will give you added insights on the advisability of writing on specific subjects. It is also a good way to get to know your instructors, to show interest in writing good papers, and to pick up good tips on what to include.

Ask Your Questions

Ask yourself "What important questions should I answer in the paper if I wish to cover the topic adequately?" This attitude will help you to determine whether your topic is too broad or too narrow. Too often students find that they would have to produce encyclopedias to cover all relevant questions adequately. If you limit yourself to a few important questions, you'll be in a better position to relax as you do research and write.

Begin your paper by indicating that you intend to deal only with specific questions. Be humble, and indicate that you recognize that there may be other significant questions but that you have chosen to limit yourself to several high-priority questions.

What if my instructor says that I have missed the important questions? What do I do then?

This possibility is why we stress talking with your instructor to determine whether or not the questions that you think are important to address yourself to are those that the instructor would like answered.

What if I am in a class of 500 and don't have access to the instructor or teaching assistant?

There are several alternatives. Find out what the experts in the field believe are the important questions. Check the most recent textbooks and journals that deal with your topic. Even new books are often several years behind the times. It is wise to go to journals that are more up to date. By looking for the experts' point of view, you are likely to get a better idea of the important questions currently being investigated.

Discuss your topic with other students in the class. You may find that they are aware of important questions that you have overlooked.

Write Your Answers

Write the answers to your questions as precisely as possible; be brief. Don't include irrelevant information that clouds the issue. Make your point, back it with sufficient examples and data, and leave it at that. Answers to questions are more believable when they are precise and well documented. Let your reader know that you have done research on the answers. Don't be afraid to quote experts in the field. The more authoritative your examples, the better you will be able to

41

convince your reader. But don't overdo it; a couple of good examples should prove your point.

Arrange Your Answers

Once you have written your answers, arrange them in order so that they build upon one another. Your next task is to connect them by writing the minimal amount of material between each answer. These transitions from answer to answer should be brief. Upon completion of the transitions, you will have written the first draft of your paper.

The steps so far:

1. Determine which questions you will answer in your paper.
2. Write an introduction describing the intent of your paper, the questions that you will answer.
3. Answer each question as precisely and authoritatively as possible; provide examples to support your position.
4. Put your answers in sequence so that they build upon one another.
5. Provide transitions from answer to answer.

Rewrite Your Paper

You are now in a position to rewrite your paper. You should

1. Make sure you have clearly indicated which question you will answer
2. Check to see that your transitions flow smoothly from answer to answer
3. Correct any grammatical, punctuation, or spelling errors
4. Rewrite or refine any answers.

Good Effort and Learning

The grade given for a paper is also influenced by three questions in the back of the instructor's mind:

1. Did the student put good effort into this paper, or was it written with the minimum possible effort?
2. Did the student learn anything, or is this paper just a collection of words?
3. Is the paper original, or has it been plagiarized?

If you can arrange to do so, glance through a large number of papers. Certain quick impressions will begin to emerge. Some students turn in papers that show very little effort. You don't have to be an instructor to see that they are trying to get away with the absolute minimum commitment of time, effort, and involvement.

Reaction: Disgust
Student Learning: None
Grade: D to C-

Some students do more work, but they lack involvement with the topic. Their approach is to check out all the books they can on the subject, sit down the night before the papers are due, and put together lists of quotations: "In 1937 C. S. Johnson said. . . . His view was criticized by Smith, who said . . . by Brown, who said . . . by Jones, who said. . . . But then in Eggland's 1949 book. . . ."

Reaction: Ho hum; a collection of second-hand ideas
Student Learning: Minimal; shows no thinking
Grade: C to B-

Once in a while a student will copy long passages from a book or article written by an expert and will turn them in as the paper. Does this approach succeed? Rarely. An article written by an expert on a subject is not anything like a paper written by a student who is trying to learn a subject. And, frankly, most instructors can spot the style and point of view in the paper as having come from a certain author.

Reaction: Plagiarism
Student Learning: Zero—and tried to cheat
Grade: F

It's human nature to consider taking shortcuts. But some efforts to save time involve high risks. The probability is high that the payoff will be the opposite of what is desired.

That's why asking and answering questions work so well. An instructor reading your paper can see that your work is *original*, that you put *good effort* into it, and that you have *learned* something.

Grammar, Spelling, and Neatness

One final set of suggestions is important. Determine whether or not your instructor requires that papers be typed. Ninety-nine of 100 instructors prefer it! If you can't type, learn quickly. It is one of the best investments any students can make.

Always be careful to follow any directions your instructor gives for footnotes, bibliographies, references, and other requirements. There is nothing worse than devoting hours to a paper, only to have it returned as incomplete. The consequence of failing to follow directions can be fatal!

It may be a pain in the neck—or wherever you prefer—to follow the requirements assigned by many instructors. It is one of the small sacrifices you must learn to make as a student. In the end, you'll probably find out that there is a good

43

reason for your instructor's request. Go along with such suggestions, and you will usually be better off, both in the grade you receive and the level of your blood pressure after completing the paper.

Above all, make sure that your spelling is up to snuff; use a dictionary whenever you're in doubt. If you find that you have serious problems in this area, you'll be wise to make an arrangement with someone to check your paper for spelling and grammatical mistakes. Regardless of the quality of your ideas, there are few things that bother instructors more than poor spelling and grammar.

It has been shown in several studies that instructors always grade papers higher when they are neat and clean and when they include good spelling and grammar. *A word to the wise:* Look sharp, at least on paper.

SHAPE UP YOUR INSTRUCTOR

Many students soon learn that instructors are not usually trained to be effective teachers. Contrary to public opinion, you needn't live with this disadvantage. Students needn't spend their time discussing the incompetence of this instructor or that teaching fellow. Rather, they can use several simple strategies for shaping their instructor's behavior. What you really want is to receive a clear definition of what your instructor wants and how he or she expects you to produce it. The student who is reluctant to take an active role in improving an instructor's performance is partly to blame for mediocre classes. If you want better teaching, you should actively work to teach your instructors what effective teaching is all about.

A Strategy for Teaching Your Teacher How To Teach

You can influence what the instructor teaches you by asking for information about important questions you want answered. Talk your questions over with other students before class, so that the instructor will see that more than one student is interested. If the instructor cannot answer the question immediately, ask if he or she will put some time into it during a future class. Most instructors are pleased to have students ask for information. Try it! Try asking questions of these types:

What is your position regarding ____ ?
How does position ____ differ from ____ ?
The text makes this distinction, but it is rather unclear. Could you clarify the
  point about ____ ?
I am not sure how this theory is related to this problem. Could you tell us how
  it does?
What do you think about ____ 's statement that ____ ?

When your instructor does something that you consider represents good teaching, let him know that you appreciate it. Rewards for effective teaching are few and far between. After a better-than-average lecture, tell the instructor as you pass by: "That was a very good lecture today. I really enjoyed it." The more you reward the instructor, the better the instruction will be!

If your instructor has an evaluation form that he passes out regularly, make sure you tell him all the strong points of the class. If you must say something negative, be sure to end with a few positive comments. Aim for the "sandwich effect." You will find that instructors respond more favorably to criticism if it is sandwiched between positive comments.

If your instructor passes out an evaluation form only at the end of the year, ask him whether or not students can pass in small slips of paper after each class so that they can comment on which things are going well and where things might be improved. Don't be afraid to ask. Most instructors are extremely interested in hearing what you have to say on a regular basis. Although many don't have enough time for personal interviews or conversations after class, a small slip of paper that can be read at the instructor's convenience will result in a good feedback system.

Pay close attention to what your instructor is saying in class. When he or she is doing things that you consider effective, be very attentive. Nod; even smile. An instructor's performance is determined by attention from students. When reactions indicate approval for certain behaviors, those behaviors will increase in frequency.

When your instructor is doing something that you consider ineffective (lecturing about trivia, telling irrelevant personal stories, and so on), act disinterested. It is important that you not reward the instructor for ineffectiveness. Your disinterest must be subtle. Once he or she is back on track, begin to look interested, nod, and smile. You'll be surprised how well instructors respond to your attention.

Remember, it is your job to let your instructor know when he or she has done a good job. If you don't, nobody else will, and you will suffer for it. A good article to read on this subject is "Little Brother Is Changing You," *Psychology Today*, September 1974.

One Final Tip

It is not necessary to play the "suffering student" game. Learning can be pleasant, and studying for exams can be handled efficiently by means of the principles we've just discussed. If you prepare well for exams, then the night before each exam you can relax and do one more very helpful thing: *Get a good night's sleep!*

CHECKLIST FOR SUCCESS

____ Practice quizzing yourself with flash cards.
____ Make up and take practice tests.
____ Practice taking tests under conditions as similar as possible to those under which you will be tested.
____ Use the test-taking techniques we have suggested on each of your tests.
____ Write papers using the question-and-answer format we have suggested.
____ Give your instructor continual feedback on the things he or she is doing well.

Setting and Achieving Your Study Goals

HOW TO SET GOALS

Why should I set goals?

You need goals so that you will know where you're going in the process of educating yourself. When you know what you want to achieve, you can set your mind to it, achieve it, and stop worrying about whether or not you'll do well in your courses. Setting goals is one of the strongest ways of motivating yourself to study efficiently and effectively.

Students who don't set specific study goals for themselves usually spend a lot of time worrying about *when* they are going to do what they have to do in order to pass their courses. If you can determine what you should study to pass a course and set up a schedule to achieve study goals, you'll be in good shape, provided that you know how to study! We've spent the first four chapters of the book on study skills. Now let's make sure you know how to set study goals and design a schedule to achieve them.

How do I figure out what my study goals should be?

First, you have to ask, "Who or what can tell me what I have to do to pass the course?" The best sources of information are usually

1. Your instructor
2. Assigned course materials

47

3. Course outlines
4. Course schedules
5. Other students
6. Class discussions
7. Student manuals and programs.

From these sources you will usually be able to tell the important tasks that you have to accomplish in order to achieve your goal of passing a course and becoming a more intelligent person.

What types of tasks are usually required of students who wish to pass courses?

1. Passing tests
2. Passing quizzes
3. Writing papers
4. Participating in class discussions and presentations
5. Completing projects.

What should I consider when scheduling my study tasks?

In addition to knowing the types of tasks that you must accomplish, you should know *how, when,* and *where* they should be accomplished.

How do I accomplish these tasks?

If through some twist of fate you've skipped the first four chapters, please go back and read them. They were written in order to teach you study skills that will help you to accomplish these tasks effectively. Now we'd like to show you how to define tasks and to set schedules that will help you to achieve course goals.

What questions should I ask when defining tasks and setting up my study schedule?

When must the tasks be completed?
How much time do I have to complete the tasks?
How much can I reasonably expect to accomplish between now and the time the tasks are due?
How can I divide up my studying so that I don't put everything off until the end?
How much should I do each day if I wish to accomplish my tasks on schedule?
Are there specific requirements for the completion of tasks—format, number of pages, references, and so on?
Where will I be required to demonstrate accomplishment of the tasks?

After answering these questions, you'll be better equipped to design an effective schedule for completing tasks. You will know where you are going, how you will get there, and how to recognize when you've arrived.

SCHEDULING TASKS TO ACHIEVE GOALS

The process of scheduling is quite simple:

1. Determine your goal.
2. Figure out what study tasks you have to perform to achieve your goal and how much time you'll have in which to complete them.
3. Plan to spend specific study periods completing the study tasks.
4. Using a graph or checklist, record your progress in completing the tasks.

Here's how to set up a schedule to achieve a goal. We shall use a model in which the student's goal is to pass an exam. Having read the first four chapters of this book, our student decides that the best way to achieve this goal is to use the technique of collecting and answering questions that are likely to be on her next exam. Here are the steps we suggest that she follow in scheduling and completing tasks that will lead to her goal.

Steps in Scheduling

Goal: *To receive a passing grade on the next test.*

Task 1: Determine the sources of test questions (textbook chapters, lecture notes, study groups, old tests, student manuals, and so on).
Task 2: Determine when and where the next test will be and what material it will cover.
Task 3: Determine how many chapters must be read between now and the test.
Task 4: Plan to read a specific number of chapters each week and to generate test questions from them.
Task 5: Plan to spend specific study periods each week generating test questions from course notes, old tests, discussion groups, friends, student manuals, and so on.
Task 6: Plan to spend specific study periods each week making and taking practice tests.
Task 7: Design checklists or graphs to record progress in collecting questions and answers, as well as taking practice tests.

USES OF RECORDING PROGRESS

Keep Yourself on Schedule

What's the purpose of using a checklist or graph to record my progress in completing tasks?

Checklists and graphs are probably the most effective means of directing your progress toward a goal. You simply define the tasks that you plan to accomplish and when you'll have time to complete them, record when each task is completed, and reward yourself for completing it on schedule. That's not so hard, and it will have a tremendous motivating effect on your performance.

Reduce Anxiety and Forgetfulness

We have found that, when students keep checklists or graphs, they have less anxiety about whether or not they're studying frequently enough. They find that, after establishing a schedule, they're more likely to study and complete tasks. Graphs and checklists serve as reminders of what must be done and when it must be accomplished.

Record and Reward Your Progress

The major suggestion that we make to the student using a checklist or graph is that she reward herself for being at places on time and accomplishing specific tasks. Our goal is to help students to establish reasonable goals and then to accomplish them. Using graphs or checklists is the best means by which most students are able to record their progress. They remind students of their responsibilities and accomplishments. They say to the student, "This is what you have to do today!" or "Congratulations for having accomplished your goal!"

Few students fall by the wayside when they have clear means of establishing goals and of recording and rewarding their progress, provided that they know how to study. If you reward yourself for completing tasks, you'll find that you are more likely to achieve your goal.

DEVELOPING CHECKLISTS

What should I include in my checklist?

Each checklist should tell you

1. What tasks should be accomplished
2. When each task should be accomplished
3. On what date you actually accomplished each task
4. Whether or not you rewarded yourself for accomplishing each task
5. Whether or not you achieved your overall goal.

Important Steps in Developing a Checklist

1. Specify each of the tasks that you must accomplish to achieve your overall goal.
2. Arrange the tasks in order of importance and according to when each is most easily accomplished.

3. Indicate next to each task when you expect to achieve it.
4. Record next to each task the actual date it has been completed.
5. Record next to each task the reward you will give yourself for having accomplished the task.
6. Record whether or not you have rewarded yourself for having accomplished the task on time.
7. Record whether or not you have rewarded yourself for having accomplished the overall goal.

What would a checklist look like for the student whose goal is passing her next test?

Figure 6 is an example of what was worked up with one student who came in for counseling.

Beverly Bailey
Introductory Psychology

Goal: To receive a passing grade on first psychology test of the semester

Exam date: September 29, 1975

Today's date: September 1, 1975

Responsibilities: Read chapters 1-5 in *Understanding Human Behavior: An Introduction to Psychology* by James V. McConnell

Take lecture notes for September 1, 3, 5, 8, 10, 12, 15, 17, 19, 22, 24, 26

Get a copy of last year's exam

Attend study group

Study Behavior	Due Date	Date Completed	Reward	Yes/No
1. Read Chapter 1, and generate questions, answers, and summary	Sept. 2			
2. Read Chapter 2 (same as 1)	Sept. 5			
3. Read Chapter 3 (same as 1)	Sept. 9			
4. Read Chapter 4 (same as 1)	Sept. 16			
5. Read Chapter 5 (same as 1)	Sept. 23			
6. Generate questions from today's lecture, and take practice quiz	Sept. 1			
7. Same as 6	Sept. 3			

51

Study Behavior	Due Date	Date Completed	Reward	Yes/No
8. Same as 6	Sept. 5			
9. Same as 6	Sept. 8			
10. Same as 6	Sept. 10			
11. Same as 6	Sept. 12			
12. Same as 6	Sept. 15			
13. Same as 6	Sept. 17			
14. Same as 6	Sept. 19			
15. Same as 6	Sept. 22			
16. Same as 6	Sept. 24			
17. Same as 6	Sept. 26			
18. Generate questions from old test	Sept. 10			
19. Make up and take practice test for Chapters 1, 2	Sept. 7			
20. Make up and take practice test for Chapters 3, 4	Sept. 17			
21. Make up and take practice test for Chapter 5	Sept. 24			
22. Make up and take practice test from all sources of questions	Sept. 27, 28			
23. Meet with study group to make up practice test	arrange			
24. Take exam	Sept. 29			
25. Achieve goal: Pass exam				

Figure 6. Model checklist.

Beverly decided to reward herself each time that she completed one of her tasks on time. She set due dates, then recorded when each task was completed and whether or not she had received her reward. It was important for her to list her rewards so that there was something to motivate her to complete her tasks on time. Too often in the past, she had found that she put everything off until the last minute and became panic-stricken when she realized how much she had to do. Now, whenever she had completed a task on time, she wrote "Yes" on the chart, indicating that she had rewarded herself for doing so.

Beverly listed a series of rewards to choose from whenever she completed a task on time. She was free to choose rewards from outside the list, but we encouraged her to develop a list that would motivate her to keep up with her studies.

Beverly's Rewards

1. Watching television
2. Reading magazine
3. Eating snack
4. Taking a nap
5. Playing cards
6. Going for a walk
7. Playing tennis
8. Calling boyfriend
9. Going on date
10. Ice-cream sundae
11. Riding bike
12. Going to a show

Beverly's list of rewards is likely quite different from one you would develop. Remember, everyone works for rewards that he values, and we encourage you to reward yourself for studying effectively, just as most people reward themselves for going to work by collecting pay checks.

Isn't it rather time consuming to make checklists? Couldn't the time be spent better studying?

The checklist in Figure 6 took Beverly fifteen minutes to make up. Once it was completed she knew what she had to do and when she had to complete each task. Afterward, she spent less time worrying about whether or not she was doing the right things and whether she was ahead of or behind schedule. The checklist was an excellent investment in the game of learning to study efficiently and effectively. You may use any type of checklist you wish. This one is simply a model with which our students have had much success.

Benefits of Developing a Checklist

What can you guarantee the checklist would have done for Beverly?

If Beverly followed the behaviors that she had outlined she would, first, have had a good set of questions, answers, and summaries for each chapter. Second, she would not have been faced with the problem of having put off reading the chapters until just before the exam. She would have studied them periodically over a month and would have finished them at least a week before the test. Third, she would have made up questions and answers immediately following her lectures and would have practiced quizzing herself to prove that she had really comprehended the lectures.

Fourth, Beverly would have taken a practice test for each chapter before she took a final practice test. Before the exam she would have been well prepared and would have had to spend less time in final review. This change has a tremendous positive effect on most students' digestive tracts and fingernails, both of which often take a beating when they wait until the last minute to figure out what will be on the next exam.

Fifth, Beverly would have found out from her friends what they thought was likely to be on the exam. Sixth, she would also have obtained a fair idea of what would be on this year's test from looking at a copy of last year's exam. Seventh, she would have been constantly reminded whether she was ahead of, keeping up with, or behind her study schedule. Eighth, she would have rewarded herself for completing each of the tasks leading to her goal of passing the exam.

Finally, Beverly would have increased her motivation to study. In fact, in talking to us about this schedule, she became so enthusiastic that she was going to do the first two chapters immediately to get a head start. She was told, however: "Don't let yourself jump ahead; only allow yourself to study for a certain amount of time. When you've finished, reward yourself, and go on to something else."

The Completed Checklist

It is interesting to compare the proposed checklist that Beverly had made out at the beginning of the month with the same checklist after she had attempted to follow her schedule of tasks and to reward herself for completing them on time (see Figures 6, 7). As you will see, she chose most of her rewards from her original list, but periodically she satisfied a whim or spur-of-the-moment desire that she hadn't included on her original list of rewards. It is important to notice that she did not have to spend a lot of money to reward herself. By choosing activities that she enjoyed but seldom found time for when going to school, she was able to encourage and reward her good study behavior while keeping herself out of debt.

Many students ask: "But what can I reward myself with? Everything costs so much." Yet they often complain that they never have time to do things they enjoy—playing cards, watching television, riding their bikes, drinking beer, and going out with their friends to enjoy the "good life." Scheduling rewards for completing tasks encourages students to partake of their favorite activities. They have no reason to feel guilty, as so many students do when they take time away from their studies. The rule of thumb is *when you earn a reward for studying, take it, and never, never cheat yourself.*

Study Behavior	Due Date	Date Completed	Reward	Yes/No
1. Read Chapter 1, and generate questions, answers, and summary	Sept. 2	Sept. 2	Hour T.V.	yes
2. Read Chapter 2 (same as 1)	Sept. 5	Sept. 5	Hour T.V.	yes
3. Read Chapter 3 (same as 1)	Sept. 9	Sept. 9	Read mags.	yes
4. Read Chapter 4 (same as 1)	Sept. 16	Sept. 16	Sundae	yes
5. Read Chapter 5 (same as 1)	Sept. 23	Sept. 23	Hour T.V.	yes
6. Generate questions from today's lecture, and take practice quiz	Sept. 1	Sept. 1	Hour nap	yes

Study Behavior	Due Date	Date Completed	Reward	Yes/No
7. Same as 6	Sept. 3	Sept. 4	None	no (late)
8. Same as 6	Sept. 5	Sept. 5	Cards	yes
9. Same as 6	Sept. 8	Sept. 8	Rode bike	yes
10. Same as 6	Sept. 10	Sept. 11	None	no (late)
11. Same as 6	Sept. 12	Sept. 12	Ice cream	yes
12. Same as 6	Sept. 15	Sept. 16	None	no (late)
13. Same as 6	Sept. 17	Sept. 17	Tennis	yes
14. Same as 6	Sept. 19	Sept. 19	Walk	yes
15. Same as 6	Sept. 22	Sept. 22	Cards	yes
16. Same as 6	Sept. 24	Sept. 24	Call friend	yes
17. Same as 6	Sept. 26	Sept. 26	Hour T.V.	yes
18. Generate questions from old test	Sept. 10	Sept. 10	Sundae	yes
19. Make up and take practice test for Chapters 1, 2	Sept. 7	Sept. 7	Show	yes
20. Make up and take practice test for Chapters 3, 4	Sept. 17	Sept. 17	Show	yes
21. Make up and take practice test for Chapter 5	Sept. 24	Sept. 24	Show	yes
22. Make up and take practice test from all sources of questions	Sept. 27, 28	Sept. 27, 28	3 hours T.V.	yes
23. Meet with study group to make up practice test	arrange	Sept. 27	Nap	yes
24. Take exam	Sept. 29	Sept. 29	Date	Yes
25. Achieve goal: Pass exam	Exam grade: 92%		Concert	yes

Figure 7. Beverly's completed checklist.

Notice that Beverly failed on several occasions to complete her tasks on time. She therefore did not reward herself. It was important that she receive the reward only when the task had been completed on time, for procrastination had been a big problem for her in the past. We decided that it was important that her chart serve as a means of encouraging her not only to complete her work but also to complete it on time.

For other students punctuality may not be a problem, and it would then not be necessary to reward themselves only if tasks were finished on time. But usually we find that, if a person begins skipping tasks or finishing them later than he had planned, he tends to return to less effective study techniques, like cramming before exams.

DEVELOPING A GRAPH

Important Steps in Developing a Graph

How can I use a graph to record my progress?

A graph is a good means of showing the achievement of tasks, which are counted as you complete them. Beverly, for example, might graph the number of questions and answers she has generated from text chapters, lecture notes, old tests, and so on.

When using a graph to record progress, how do I determine whether or not I've reached my goal?

Beverly's goal was to pass her test. She knew that, if she predicted and answered questions, she was likely to pass it. She asked herself, "How many questions and answers should I generate from lecture notes, chapters, and other sources to ensure that I comprehend the material and pass the test?"

If she had developed fifteen questions for each chapter and six for each lecture, she would have had 147 questions and answers at the end of four weeks. She would have distributed her work as follows:

Week	Chapters	Lectures	Total Questions
1	1, 2	1–3	48
2	3	4–6	33
3	4	7–9	33
4	5	10–12	33
			147

In making her graph, Beverly would put the number of tasks she had to accomplish on the vertical line. On the bottom, or horizontal, line she would list the amount of time she had to accomplish her tasks. The graph would look like Figure 8.

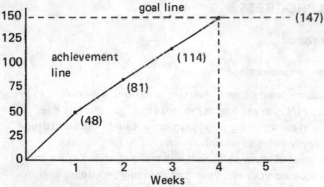

Figure 8. A model graph of questions and answers.

Achievement and Goal Lines

Beverly's goal line is drawn in Figure 8; it shows her four-week goal, 147 questions and answers. Had she achieved the goal before four weeks were up, she would have crossed the goal line and continued to develop questions and answers. Most important, she would have known that she had accomplished her goal.

The achievement line is drawn in Figure 8 to show the rate at which Beverly had to accomplish her tasks if she wished to reach her goal in four weeks. As she recorded her progress, she would see whether she was ahead of, keeping up with, or behind schedule. If she were behind, she would know it was time to get moving. If she were ahead of or on schedule, she could relax and turn to other activities.

Note: The tasks that you must accomplish (number of questions and answers, problems solved, pages read, pages written, and so on) are always listed along the vertical line. The amount of time you have in which to complete the tasks is always written across the bottom line.

Benefits of Graphing

How would the graph help Beverly to reach her goal of passing the test?

The graph will tell her how well she is predicting and answering questions that are likely to be on her test. She'll know how much time she has to complete her tasks and how many should be completed each week. She'll know whether she is ahead of or behind schedule. The achievement line serves this purpose. She'll be able to record her progress as soon as she completes each task. Finally and most important, though often overlooked, is that the graph will encourage her to reward herself for working to meet her goal.

57

REWARDING YOUR PROGRESS

The Importance of Rewards

Why is rewarding myself so important?

Most students try to escape from or avoid aversive situations. They want to get the pressure off of themselves, finish reading the stupid book, get the test over with, and keep from flunking out or doing poorly. In our estimation, this attitude is tragic. Students should enjoy going to school.

We have shown you a series of study skills that will make studying more enjoyable. We would like to increase your enjoyment of studying and doing well in school by encouraging you to reward yourself for accomplishing tasks and achieving goals.

Students often say: "Well, isn't rewarding myself bribery? Why should I reward myself for something I have to do?" The answer is simple: You're more likely to do what's good for you when you encourage yourself to do it. We suggest rewarding yourself with free time, television time, reading magazines, or whatever you enjoy. The rewards need not cost anything. They may simply be opportunities to engage in activities that you enjoy. Go ahead and give yourself periodic rewards for accomplishing tasks.

Guidelines for the Use of Graphs, Checklists, and Rewards

Okay, I'll give the graph and checklist a try. Are there any special rules I should follow in using them?

Yes. We'd suggest, first, that you always *post* your graphs or checklists where they will be visible. They can then serve as constant reminders of what you should be doing and how well you are doing it.

Second, ask yourself what you should really be able to do in the amount of time you have to accomplish your goal. *Schedule* your work, as we suggested earlier, so that all the work for a particular course isn't crammed into a short period of time. Spread it out, so that you have time to relax before the test or the date your paper is due.

Third, list the rewards that you will receive for accomplishing goals for yourself. Always reward yourself as you accomplish your goals! Never cheat yourself!

The response from our students throughout the years to using checklists, schedules, and graphs has been exceedingly favorable. They have enjoyed the benefits of having more predictable study schedules. Needless to say, they've also enjoyed their rewards. Equally important, they have seen improvements in their grades. If you'd like the same results, we encourage you to give these tactics a try.

Characteristics of Successful, Unsuccessful, and Not Successful Students

SELF-DEVELOPMENT PROJECTS

Up to this point we have emphasized those behaviors that can significantly improve your success in school. We have described many tested, practical methods for acquiring those behaviors and have explained the underlying principles.

Now our focus will shift to helping you be a successful *person* in school. We shall be looking at many attitudes, traits, and behaviors that can be learned. Throughout this and the following chapters, you will find self-development projects. Each SDP includes tips and guidelines on how to acquire the traits or behaviors discussed. The projects include

Gaining a more positive attitude
The value of tracking positives
Discussing this book
Questioning your career
Increasing your achievement motivation
How to be self-actualizing
Visualizing a successful you
Rating your survivor traits
Guidelines for starting friendships
Guidelines for successful friendships.

Keep in mind, however, that there is much more here than any one person can handle all at once. Limit yourself to one or two of the most interesting projects at first. Hold off trying others until you have the first ones done.

"Hi, Lisa. Can we sit here?"

"Hi, Kyle. Sure. Here, I'll move my pack. Hi, Terry."

"We just got our grades. Terry and I got Cs in English. What did you get, Lisa?"

"I got an A."

"Good! You got what you were aiming for. I tried for a B but missed it by a few points."

"That's too bad."

"Sometimes I wonder if I should try so hard. Maybe Terry's way is better. He doesn't sweat it. Right, Terry? He just reads the text, goes to class, takes the exams, and waits to see what grade he gets. It sure is less frustrating."

SUCCESS IN REACHING YOUR GOALS

A student's grades should not be assumed to be indicators of how successful he or she is. Success means reaching a goal. So people who don't set goals are neither successful nor unsuccessful. There are thus three possible states:

1. Being successful
2. Being unsuccessful
3. Being neither successful nor unsuccessful.

In the group introduced Lisa is successful, Kyle unsuccessful, and Terry neither successful nor unsuccessful. There are those who try and make it, those who try but don't make it, and those who don't try.

Why make this distinction? For several reasons. First, success is measured in terms of the goals you set, not in terms of the grades you receive. For a student whose aim is to have a B average, a B average is success. Second, the person who is unsuccessful may be in the habit of aiming for high goals and falling short. Or he may be in the process of learning how to be more successful. For him this kind of effort is new, and not reaching the goal means being "not successful *yet*."

The person who is not trying may have never thought of setting goals. Others don't set goals because the possibility of not reaching them and thus experiencing failure is something they don't want to risk. They fear failure and they can't fail if they don't set goals.

All together, we can see that there are many different reasons why a student may not be experiencing much success. For most students, however, the main reason for less success than they could have is too little time spent setting goals for themselves. As you read through these chapters, keep in mind that people who achieve success over and over again are people who usually

1. Set challenging but attainable goals that they sincerely want to reach
2. Examine the possible blocks and barriers to reaching the goals
3. Look for ways to get around the blocks, increase their abilities, and get help from useful resources

61

4. Devise realistic, flexible plans for reaching goals
5. Act in ways that maximize chances of reaching the goals and minimize chances of not reaching them.

As each student begins from a different starting point, has goals different from those of others, has different strengths and weaknesses, and has different barriers to overcome, each must follow a different route to success. We shall now turn our attention to *things to take into account while figuring out the best way to be more successful.*

BEHAVIORS

Let's look first at what actions are likely to lead to success and to reduce chances of success. In a study reported by H. C. Lindgren, it was found that attendance in class made an important difference between students with high grades and students with low grades. A comparison of grade averages and class attendance showed these percentages:

Class Attendance	% Students with B Average or Higher	% Students with C– Average or Lower
Always or almost always present	85	48
Sometimes absent	8	8
Often absent	8	45

Without speculating about underlying motives or attitudes for the moment, let's focus on behavior alone. The percentages in the table suggest that attending class always or almost always helps to maximize chances of success. For the student who is often absent the percentages work in the direction of low grades.

What about the fact that 48 percent of the C– or lower students are always or almost always present?

The answer is that no one factor alone accounts for success. Success results from *many* behaviors together. Recall, for example, our discussion of note taking. We observed the behavior of students in class and saw that the ones most likely to make good grades were the ones who took notes.

Is that all it takes? Attending class regularly and taking notes?

Attending class and taking notes are only parts of the series of behaviors that lead to better grades. Lindgren's study also revealed differences in scheduling study time:

Type of Schedule	% Students with B Average or Higher	% Students with C– Average or Lower
Detailed, strict	38	38
Loose, flexible	30	5
None	32	57

Why do you favor filling out a detailed study schedule when 32 percent of the better students say they have no study schedule?

Many students who get high grades *study all the time.* Such a student doesn't need a schedule. He is also a student who seldom dates, participates in sports, or has much time to spend with friends. The whole purpose of this book is to show that, by scheduling and using time in an intelligent way, a person can have higher grades and *still* have time for all these other things. Of the students with low grades, 57 percent admit that they have no study schedules and spend very little time studying.

Okay. So it makes sense that more than 50 percent of the students who have low grades have no study schedules and don't study much. But what about the 38 percent who have strict schedules and still have low grades?

Here is where we have to look at the behaviors that occur during actual study time. As we have discussed in the first five chapters, our experience is that many students with poor grades are expending energy but are not getting results. They are spending time on the books but not obtaining any learning that pays off for them. Notice that we are not saying that students with low grades don't learn anything. Many learn about things that interest them, but they aren't studying to pass tests. Here is where we find the key difference. The students with high grades study to pass tests. They spend their study time asking and answering questions likely to be on exams. That's why we have stated several times that, if you are not studying to pass tests, you are not studying to be successful in school.

Aren't you overemphasizing studying to get good grades?

No. Just the opposite. You can do anything with your life and your mind that you want to. And that's okay. We are saying that, *if* you choose to be more successful as a student, there is an intelligent way to accomplish this goal without having to study all the time. We are also saying that you shouldn't study too much. It is best for you to arrange to have time for doing other things.

You can see better what we mean by looking at the percentage of students who use flexible schedules. Notice that only 5 percent of the students with low grades report using such schedules, whereas 30 percent of the students with high grades use them. Why the big difference? Because developing a schedule works. Many of the students with high grades who use flexible schedules or who schedule their time loosely have started with stricter schedules. Not all, of course. Some are fairly unorganized people who have recognized the need for some kind of schedule and have found that loose schedules are the best they can manage. But often the person has first learned the value of scheduling by working out a detailed plan and then, as scheduling time became a habit, gradually slipped into a looser, less rigid one.

Our picture of the behaviors of students who get high grades and still have time for friends and activities is that they attend class always or almost always, take lecture notes, have some kind of study schedule that limits the amount of time they spend studying, and use their limited study time to ask and answer questions likely to be on tests.

The reason we keep coming back to the study schedule is that we see it as the best way to keep yourself from studying too much. It helps you to stop wasting time that could be better devoted to other activities.

TIME MANAGEMENT

We have said previously that learning how to be successful in school is only part of learning how to be successful in life. This idea of using a schedule to *limit* how much time you spend studying is a good example of what we are getting at.

One of the most important steps you can take toward being in control of your own life is to learn how to be in control of your time. There are always more things to do than you have time to do. It doesn't matter so much whether the schedule is loose or detailed as long as the objective is being accomplished.

As there are more things to do than you have time to do, you must make choices. You make many choices during a day; for example, "It's time for lunch, but I might as well keep on with this math as long as I'm into it." Your decisions are easier if you have set some priorities. Many decisions are between high-priority and low-priority activities: "It's an hour until dinner. Should I study for the history exam tomorrow or sew the button back on my shirt?"

Sometimes a person doesn't even realize that a choice has been made. There is always the alternative of *not* doing something. Everything you do you have chosen to do in preference to not doing it. Once you realize this fact, it is useful to form the habit of quickly asking yourself: "Must I do this?" "Is there something more important that I could be doing?" or "What would happen if I didn't do this?"

One of the keys to getting things done is to be in control of your time. Effective people make choices about time. They know that it is scarce, and so they devote it to important things. Ineffective people have poor control of their time. They often run out of it; it slips away from them. And they don't know where their time goes.

The amount of time you have available is limited, just as is the amount of money you have. You can count on a certain amount coming in each week, as you can count on an allowance or a pay check, but there is never any extra you can ask for. That's why setting up a schedule is like setting up a budget. You are deciding in advance what activities to spend your time on.

But at the start of this book you said students should spend time doing what they please!

Right! That's exactly the point of this discussion. If you schedule your time, you can plan on having blocks of it for just messing around. Call it "free time" or "personal time" if you wish. It is time you have reserved just for you, and you spend it just as you would spend pocket money or "mad" money you have set aside. By scheduling your time, you are allotting it to *all* the important things.

64

CONDUCT YOUR OWN SURVEY

How about finding out for yourself what the picture looks like? Figure 9 is an interview form that you can use as a guide to asking students how they account for their success or lack of success in school. We recommend that you interview each person, rather than asking people to give you written responses. Even though this book is copyrighted, we grant you permission to reproduce the form as you wish.

By the way, if you write up your report, will you send us a copy? Our address is on the feedback sheet at the end of this book.

ATTITUDES

Most students are aware of how good study habits can help them get higher grades, but few students are aware of how important some other kinds of habits are. They are the habits called *attitudes*.

Attitudes are mental and emotional habits, and, like all habits, they are learned. Also, like other habits, they occur without conscious effort. Because they are learned, you can do something about counterproductive attitudes that work against your reaching your goals.

We often find with students who are getting grades lower than they would like to have that the conscious desire to do better is present but that some unconscious attitudes work against it.

Can you do anything about this problem? Yes. William James, one of the first psychologists, said that the greatest discovery of his time was that, by changing your attitudes, you can change your life.

The first step we have to take is to find out your attitude toward the idea that you can do anything about how things go for you. Take several minutes right now to go through the attitude survey in Figure 10.

Scoring Your Survey: How "Internal" Are You?

To score yourself, add up the number of choices you have selected on the left-hand side of Figure 10. This total is your "internal" score. Students who took this test during the pretesting of the book received scores ranging from 6 to 12. The higher your "internal" score, the greater the control you see yourself as having over your life.

Psychologist Julian Rotter discovered that students show some extreme differences in attitude toward whether or not they can exert much control over what happens in their lives. Students who know that they are personally responsible for many things that happen in their lives are called "internalizers." They believe that the main location of what controls important forces in their lives is inside themselves.

Many other students believe that they are the helpless pawns of fate, that the forces influencing their lives are all outside themselves. These students are called "externalizers" by Rotter.

Name of person interviewed:

Date:

Interview Conditions:

Grade Average of Person:

What reasons would you say account for your success (or lack of success) in school?

What kinds of goals are you working toward?

Which of the following is most descriptive of you in regard to class attendance?
Always or almost always attend _____
Sometimes absent   _____
Often absent   _____

Do you take lecture notes?
Always   _____
Usually   _____
Rarely   _____

Do you budget your study time? Do you make decisions about what you will and won't put your time into?

What kind of study schedule do you have?
Detailed, strict   _____
Loose, flexible   _____
None   _____

When you study do you focus on trying to identify questions most likely to be on the exams?
Always   _____
Frequently   _____
Sometimes   _____

Other questions:

Figure 9. Student-interview form.

From each pair of alternatives below select the one that most closely represents your personal belief.

1. ____ Promotions are earned through hard work and persistence.   ____ Promotions usually come from having the right people like you.

2. ____ How hard I study determines the grades I get.   ____ I would get better grades if the teaching in this school were better.

3. ____ The increasing divorce rate indicates that fewer people are trying to make their marriages last.   ____ Fate determines how long a marriage will last. All you can do is hope your partner will stay with you for life.

4. ____ When I want to, I can usually get others to see things my way.   ____ It is useless to try to change another person's opinions or attitudes.

5. ____ In our society a person's income is determined largely by ability.   ____ Finding a well-paying job is a matter of being luckier than the next guy.

6. ____ If I handle people right, I can usually influence them.   ____ I have very little ability to influence people.

7. ____ My grades are a result of my effort; luck has little to do with it.   ____ Whether I study or not has little effect on the grades I get.

8. ____ People like me can change the course of world events by making ourselves heard.   ____ It is wishful thinking to believe that one can influence what happens in society at large.

9. ____ I am the master of my fate.   ____ When I see an unfortunate person, I sometimes think "There but for the grace of God go I."

10. ____ Getting along with people is a skill that can be learned.   ____ Most people are difficult to get along with, and there is no use trying to be friendly.

11. ____ I am usually a good influence on others.   ____ Running around with bad company leads a person into bad ways.

12. ____ Peace of mind comes from learning how to adapt to life's stresses.   ____ I would be much happier if people weren't so irritating.

Figure 10. Attitude survey.

67

The interesting point is that both kinds of student are correct, for each of these attitudes is self-maintaining. The students who are high "internals" believe they can influence much of what happens to them, so they take actions to make things happen, and the results of their efforts confirm their beliefs. Students who are high "externals" seldom take action because they believe that it won't do any good, and sure enough most of what happens to them is determined by outside forces and other people.

Positive and Negative

Much of what we have said here about "internals" and "externals" fits with the more commonly used terms "positive" and "negative attitudes."
People with positive attitudes tend to

Look for the good in a situation
Be optimistic about outcomes
Be happy about whatever good things are happening
Be pleasant people to be around
Be rarely sidetracked by irritations
Focus on getting good results.

People with negative attitudes tend to

Find something wrong in any situation
Be pessimistic about outcomes
Be unhappy because some good things haven't happened
Believe things will eventually get bad
Be easily distracted by irritations
Be unpleasant to be around
Focus on having had good intentions.

We want to explain, however, that we do not have a negative attitude toward people with negative attitudes. For one thing, people with negative attitudes make people with positive attitudes look good. Having a negative attitude is a characteristic some people have. And there are many advantages to having a negative attitude. If there weren't any advantages, no one would stay that way long!
Some advantages are

You can frustrate people who would like to influence you.
People don't expect as much of you.
You get more attention.
The world is more predictable.
It's easier than being positive.
You avoid disappointment.
Your mind works to help you avoid responsibility for things that go wrong.
Having fun playing games with people.

68

How do you know if you have a positive or a negative attitude? If you don't know, then you probably tend to be negative. People with positive attitudes usually know that they have them. A person maintains a positive attitude pretty much out of choice. He is consciously aware of the existence of the attitude and how desirable it is to maintain it. People who are in the middle (neither strongly positive nor strongly negative) or who tend to be negative usually have not thought much about attitudes.

Consistent with what we have said about "externalizers," people with negative attitudes rarely entertain the idea that they can do anything about the attitudes they have. As one rather negative student said, "An attitude is an attitude, and you're stuck with what you've got."

We ran across several examples of attitudes when we passed our earlier drafts of this book. A student with a positive attitude said: "Hey! Good! Maybe I can get more tips in how to do better in chemistry." A student with a negative attitude said, "Well, I can try some of these things, but they probably won't work with me."

A positive person tends to be looking for ways to improve. There is the desire to be better and awareness that a person can learn to be better. A negative person isn't as oriented toward learning and improvement. If urged to do something by external forces (other people), he or she may promise to "try." The promise "I'll try" usually signifies that the person will go through the motions for a while but expects eventually to drift back into acting as he always has.

Another key difference is whether or not you learn from experience. A person with a positive attitude has a positive attitude toward mistakes. As one scientist wrote: "If your experiment does exactly as predicted, you don't learn anything. The times when you learn something are those times when your experiment does not go as predicted."

A person with a positive attitude is unhappy about making a mistake or not reaching a goal, but he soon starts thinking to himself, "What will I do the next time it happens?" He thinks:

The next time I get asked a question like that . . . .
The next time she says that I'm going to say . . . .
The next time I do something stupid like that . . . .

The positive person tends to focus on the future.

A negative person tends to dwell on the past. He spends a lot of time feeling sorry for himself:

I would be able to study if I didn't have such a gabby roommate.
I could probably do better in English if my high-school teacher had taught me something.
I thought I would like psych, but the instructor bores me to death.

Do you recognize any of these mental habits in yourself? If you recognize some of the negative statements as similar to ones you make, we hope you have also recognized by now that you have a choice about how you allow your mind to react.

All these reactions are *learned*. Successful people work at acquiring positive mental habits.

Let's take the example of the boring instructor. If you are turned off by a course because you don't like the instructor, you are allowing your mind to ask the wrong question. You are letting your mind ask, "Do I like him?" The right question is "Does he know his subject?" Whether or not he happens to have good speaking skills is irrelevant to your obtaining useful information about the subject.

For the student with a positive attitude, a boring instructor may offer a good opportunity to practice the techniques we described in the section on shaping your instructor (see Chapter 4).

We don't want to mislead you into thinking that a person has to change his attitude before his performance will improve. There is ample evidence to show that the opposite is often true. After first changing performance, he finds that his attitude slowly changes.

William James was one of the first to discover that changed attitudes can change behavior and that changed behavior can change attitudes. More recently, Frederick Herzberg has been successful in showing managers how to improve workers' attitudes through job enrichment. Many managers believe that workers do poor work because of their poor attitudes. Herzberg's approach is to improve attitudes by giving people more meaningful work. He believes very strongly that poor attitudes are a consequence of simple, dull, boring jobs.

SDP: Gaining a More Positive Attitude

Here is a four-week plan for gaining a more positive attitude:

1. Glance back at the lists of examples of positive and negative attitudes for a moment.
2. Make up your own lists of positive behaviors that you would like to acquire and negative behaviors that you want to eliminate.

Positive thoughts, statements, feelings, actions	Negative thoughts, statements, feelings, actions

3. Get a pack of 3 x 5-inch cards. Each day for the next twenty-eight days carry a card with you. As you go through the day, record each time that you do, say, or think something you feel is a sign of having a positive attitude. On the other side of the card record signs of having a negative attitude.

4. Each night record on a chart the number of positive behaviors and the number of negative behaviors for that day. Students using this program have been able to increase greatly their positive behaviors and to decrease their negative behaviors.

Note: As you go through this program you will find more behaviors to add to your original lists, so feel free to revise them as you go along.

ENVIRONMENTS

Maintaining a positive attitude can be difficult if one is in a negative environment. And as strongly as you may be motivated to be successful, there are always a number of *un*motivators working on you.

Some of the *un*motivators reported by good students:

Expenditure of more energy
Harder work than poor students
Risk of failure
Less time with friends than poor students
Less chance to loaf
Missing some good things because of studying for assignments or tests
People expecting more ("You get a B, and they have a heart attack!)
Inability to go out for sports as often because practice interferes with studying
Greater likelihood of being razzed and called "bookworm" or "egghead"
People giving you a bad time if your grades drop a little.

To this list of *un*motivators we add

Input overload—being exposed to too much information too fast
Delayed reinforcement—the real payoff for learning is far away and not clearly outlined; grades are temporary motivators and not the end goal
Required courses with large enrollments—"Why are you taking history?" "Because it is listed in the catalogue as a required course."
Majors with uncertain career value—"What can you do with a degree in _____ if you don't go to graduate school?" "I don't know. They said I had to declare a major, and _____ seemed as good as any."
Required electives—"Why are you taking psych?" "I need some hours in social sciences as a requirement for my major."
Families who don't care if you do well—"Hey look, Dad! I went from a B- to an A- average!" "So?"
Peer-group norms—If you get top grades, some people you like may reject you.

All these unmotivators help to show why so few students are highly successful. It isn't easy. There are many forces working against it, and that is exactly why we included these lists. Glance back for a moment to the point early in this chapter

71

where we listed steps taken by successful people. Notice that they "examine the possible blocks and barriers." What this statement means is that, if you are truly serious about being more successful, then a practical step is to spend some time examining all the forces working against your being successful. If it were easy to be successful, more students would be.

So what can be done?

If you make yourself aware of all the forces working against you, you will be better prepared to hold up against them. Thinking about all the possible problems and difficulties before you experience them prepares you better for handling them.

Psychologist Irving Janis did a study of hospital patients in which he found that patients who worried a little bit about the pain and problems they would have after surgery were able to handle them much better than other patients were. So, it is healthy to worry a little bit. When worry becomes self-defeating is when it prevents you from taking action or makes you so nervous you can't function well.

We have some specific suggestions about techniques you should consider in your approach to these problems. In our opinion, one of the most serious problems is lack of support, encouragement, and recognition from people who are important to you. And, let's face it, there are some students who have been working so hard at getting good grades they don't have many friends. They haven't had any time for friends.

What can be done about getting more support from others? First, don't be so quick to talk about your accomplishments with people who are going to be negative. If you have friends who give you a bad time when you excuse yourself to study, then ask yourself about the purpose of friendships. Are your "friends" forcing you to make a choice between being liked by them now and your future success? Ask yourself: "Ten years from now what do I want life to be like? Ten years from now who would I like my friends to be? Will my closest friends still be these same people?"

If people in your family are the ones who give you negative comments or don't care about what you accomplish, use some of the principles for shaping your instructor that we described in Chapter 4. Here is an example of how successful this approach can be.

Barbara was about to start her sophomore year of nursing school when she took introductory psychology during a summer session. As one of her class assignments she was required to do a "behavior-modification project." The project was not to be carried out in a laboratory; the idea was to apply the principles of behavior modification to a person or animal she had frequent contact with in daily life.

Other students in the class went to work on younger sisters, family dogs or cats, neighbor children, bus drivers, talkative roommates, boy friends who drove too fast, smokers, overweight friends, and other available subjects. Barbara decided to use her father as the subject for her project.

Barbara's relationship with her father was very poor. She said:

We were always looking for ways to cut each other. He enjoyed saying rotten things about nurses to me. If he'd say "good morning" to me, I'd say "what's good about it!" If I came home from school excited about something and wanted to talk about it, he would just sit there in his chair and keep on reading. He didn't care about anything that was happening to me. Once when I was trying to talk to him about school he got up and walked out of the room. Didn't say a word. Just walked out.

He is retired, so he is usually home during the day. I know he likes it, if I'm home at lunch time, if I make a bowl of soup for him. I'd go into the kitchen and make myself something. He would get his hopes up and then be disappointed when he saw I only fixed something for myself. Chocolate cake is his favorite, so when I baked something I made sure it was *not* chocolate cake.

When we were assigned the project, I decided to see if I could improve my life at home. It is hard enough getting through nursing school without always having a big hassle at home. I've been dreaming about going into nursing for a long time. It's exciting! I wanted my family to *care!"*

Barbara's Plan for Changing Her Father

Barbara decided that each time her father responded pleasantly or positively she would be pleasant to him and do something special to show her appreciation for his interest in her. The slightest positive gesture from him would be immediately attended to by her. She would try never to overlook the slightest improvement, no matter how small or weak. Her goal was to increase the number of times her father showed interest in her and the depth of his interest.

Following the procedure recommended in class, Barbara outlined these steps:

Desired project goal: Father to greet me cheerfully each morning; show interest in what is happening at school; talk with me about school
Current level of desired behavior: Seldom looks at me or listens when I am talking about school; never asks about school
Reinforcements to father for increase in desired behavior: Bowl of soup at lunch; bake cookies and chocolate cake; smile and say "Thanks for talking with me"; kiss on the cheek.

Three weeks later Barbara reported the results of her project to the class:

My first chance to use a reinforcement was during a lunch time. I talked with Dad for several minutes, and he listened without looking at his magazine. I didn't try to push my luck by going on too long, so I got up and asked him if he would like for me to fix him a bowl of soup. His face brightened up. He smiled and said, "Sure."

In the morning if he said "hello" to me, I'd smile and say "Hello" and kiss him on the cheek. Mornings are much more pleasant now.

After about three times fixing him soup at lunch, he began showing more interest and would ask questions. Then one evening he asked me to tell him about a book I read, and we spent almost twenty minutes talking. I immediately got up and went out to the kitchen and baked him a batch of cookies.

Last Friday afternoon I got home about 1:30. He got up from his chair as soon as he heard me come in and came over and said: "I've been waiting for you. I would like to know more about what you are doing in school if you have time to talk." Did I ever! We spent *two hours* talking. That is the longest my father has had a conversation with me in my whole life! It was great! He was *really* interested. When we finished I gave him a big hug, said how great it was talking with him, and went out and baked him a chocolate cake.

73

Barbara suddenly grew quiet. Her eyes started to water, and she struggled to hold back tears. Her voice choked up a little as she went on to say: "Something happened this morning that isn't in my written report. I was getting ready to leave for school and Dad came up and put his arm around me. He said, 'Barbara, I want to take you out to dinner next week. I want to get to know you better before it's too late.' "

SDP: The Value of Tracking Positives

We are often bothered by the actions of others, yet we believe there is no observable way of stopping those actions. Research into the principles of reinforcement suggests that often we may unknowingly be reinforcing undesirable actions in others simply by paying attention to them. It is important to learn to ignore undesirable behaviors and to pay attention to those desirable behaviors that are exactly opposite to the undesirable actions. By encouraging the desirable behaviors, we may prevent the undesirable ones.

For example, your roommate may talk consistently about the terrible weather, scarcity of money, the difficulties of going to school, and dozens of other nauseating topics. Granted that life is rough, but there is little you can do about it at the moment. What you really want is that your roommate be pleasant and not dwell on all the negative aspects of life. Here's how you do it.

STEP 1
Your goal is to increase the number of pleasant things your roommate says and to decrease the number of unpleasant remarks.

STEP 2
Your method is to reinforce pleasant talk and to ignore irritating talk. For example, when your roommate says things that you think are positive, you should pay close attention, maintain eye contact, nod in agreement, smile, comment favorably, and generally encourage him to talk about pleasant topics.

When your roommate says things that you consider negative, you should be inattentive, look away, try to remain expressionless, and—most important—say nothing if at all possible. To extinguish negative behavior it is important that you not do things that tend to reinforce it. You must thus not provide the attentive behavior that usually reinforces this type of verbal output.

STEP 3
Recording the behavior of your roommate is important to your project. During certain periods of time each day, record for fifteen minutes the number of positive comments your roommate makes and the number of negative comments. The comments should be graphed each day, which will allow you to see your progress in reinforcing positive comments and extinguishing negative ones.

EXTINCTION

Remember, behavior increases or decreases as a result of the consequence of that behavior. If you wish to extinguish a behavior, you must not allow it to be followed by something that reinforces it. Most people are reinforced for griping because other people listen to them. Even if you tell them to stop griping, you will often find that they continue to do so because they receive attention whenever they gripe.

REINFORCEMENT

Getting rid of griping behavior isn't enough. You can't expect a person to give up talking completely! It is thus your job to reinforce your roommate every time he or she says something positive. You will speed up the extinction of negative talk when you reinforce talk that is incompatible with the negative; it's hard to frown when you're smiling.

STEP 4

You should analyze your performance after several days of working toward your goal. If the graph shows that your roommate's negative comments are decreasing and that his positive comments are increasing, then you are likely reinforcing pleasant talk and ignoring negative talk.

Remember, griping behavior is likely to be resistant to extinction if it has been reinforced intermittently. It is important that you ignore every negative instance and attend closely to what you want to hear.

If the behavior does not decrease after several weeks, it is likely that you are periodically reinforcing it. If there are other people living with you, they must act in ways consistent with your project; otherwise they will delay your success.

Be careful to look for a trend in the initial stage of your graph. When you begin withholding attention for the griping behavior, it is likely to increase. Do not be alarmed. Continue ignoring negatives and attending to positives. The more you attend to positives, the more rapidly the negatives will drop off.

Students have succeeded in using this project to increase such behaviors as arriving on time for dates, smiling, eating nourishing foods, and keeping quiet during study hours.

CREATE YOUR OWN JUNTO

If your present group of friends does not support your efforts to be more successful, you might consider the advantages of associating with people who will support you. You may discover that it is easier to find new friends who have the qualities you need than it is to change your old friends.

This suggestion about forming a junto comes from Benjamin Franklin. He used the word "junto" in the original sense—a group of people meeting for a secret purpose. In modern times "junta" has tended also to mean that the secret purpose is political and revolutionary.

The secret purpose of Franklin's junto was self-improvement. He saw that it would be very good for his self-development to meet regularly with others who, like himself, had a strong desire to better themselves. In his autobiography he wrote about how successful this approach was:

Our club, the Junto, was found so useful and afforded such satisfaction to the members that several were desirous of introducing their friends, which could not well be done without exceeding what we had settled as a convenient number, viz., twelve. We had from the beginning made it a rule to keep our institution a secret, which was pretty well observed.

The purpose in keeping secrecy and limiting the number was "to avoid the applications of improper persons for admittance, some of whom we might find it difficult to refuse." When members wanted to bring in others, Franklin suggested that they form their own separate clubs.

Reference Groups

Nowadays, more than 200 years later, social psychologists are studying the strong effects that "reference groups" have on each of us. Reference groups consist of people whose opinions and values we use as a frame of reference. We act in ways that are consistent with what they approve of. We avoid doing things that they disapprove of.

In either case, whether you think in terms of finding a new reference group or of forming a secret self-improvement junto, the basic principle is the same. The people you associate with will have a strong influence on your motivation to better yourself.

Note also that what we are describing here is a step beyond forming the study group described earlier. A study group is temporary (for the length of the course), is restricted to other students in the course, and focuses exclusively on learning answers to questions most likely to be on exams.

Your betterment group may be made up of people selected from your study groups. In five study groups that you participate in there may be two people that have the kind of openness to learning and thinking that you respond to. You may not be friends with them, but you do have pleasant rapport. These people would be those you could start having lunch with and associating with. (There will be more about how to develop friendships in Chapter 8.)

We recommend that, if you start such a group, you discuss what you want your group to do and what procedures to follow when adding new members. We also suggest that you do not elect officers and that you do not have any group project other than the common goals of individual growth and development.

SDP: Discuss This Book

A good way to start a self-improvement group is to organize a rap session about this book. Get together with four or five other students who are reading and using it. What projects have they carried out? What results have they achieved? What have they found to be of most value?

LEARNING HAS ITS OWN REWARDS

As you know, learning can be an exciting and enjoyable experience. What we have been describing in much of this book is how to get past all the blocks, barriers, handicaps, attitudes, and environmental conditions that may hold you back and how to maximize your learning by setting up as many forces as possible to help yourself. The solving of a problem, the dawning of an insight can be an exciting experience.

Archimedes, for example, struggled for a long time with a problem. The emperor needed a way to determine whether or not a gold crown was made of pure gold. Some objects presented as made of pure gold were actually debased with other metals. Archimedes pondered this problem for a long while. He knew the solution was not merely to weigh the crown because its volume had also to be known. Trying to calculate the exact amount of metal in intricate objects was hopeless.

One day, as he settled down in a bathtub brim full of water, he noticed that the deeper he settled into the tub, the more water spilled out. His body was displacing water.

He shouted "Eureka!" and jumped out of the tub. "Eureka!" he yelled, as he ran to the palace as fast as he could. He was so excited about his discovery that he didn't realize he was still naked. He had discovered what is now called the Law of Specific Gravity. He had realized that, as metals have different weights, all he had to do was to find out how much water the crown displaced in proportion to its weight, and he could calculate the purity of its gold content.

For Archimedes, learning was exciting and rewarding. Learning in school can also be more exciting than may seem possible to you. Our goal is to increase your success at learning and to help you discover new ways to be successful with less effort and greater enjoyment. Samuel Johnson once said, "Knowledge always desires increase; it is like a fire, which must first be kindled by some external agent, but which will afterwards propagate itself."

The rewards that come from learning how to learn are far beyond what most students grasp at the beginning.

CHECKLIST FOR SUCCESS

_____ Set challenging but realistic goals.
_____ List the possible blocks and barriers.
     _____ Behavioral
     _____ Attitudinal
     _____ Environmental
_____ Outline ways to overcome or get around the blocks (include careful reviews of Chapters 1–6).
     _____ Behavioral
     _____ Attitudinal
     _____ Environmental

_____ Devise a realistic, flexible plan for reaching goals.

_____ Acts in ways that maximize the chances of reaching the goals and minimize the chances of not reaching the goals.

REFERENCES AND SUGGESTED READING

Alan Lakein. *How To Get Control of Your Time and Your Life.* (New York: New American Library, 1973).

Henry Clay Lindgren. *The Psychology of College Success: A Dynamic Approach.* (New York: Wiley, 1969).

Benjamin Franklin. *Autobiography and Other Writings*, ed. by Russel B. Nye. (Boston: Houghton Mifflin, 1958).

Julian B. Rotter. "External and Internal Control," *Psychology Today* (June 1971).

How To Be
a More Successful Person

NOTICE: VOLUNTEERS WANTED

Clinical-psychology graduate students taking a course in projective testing need volunteers to take psychological tests. Inquire at the clinical-psychology office for more information.

Erik stopped and read the notice. He stood thinking for a moment and then went to sign up for the testing. After the testing was over, he made an appointment to come back and talk about the results.

"Hi, Erik. Have a seat."

"Thanks." Erik sat down and leaned forward eagerly.

"Erik, I went over the test results with my testing supervisor to make sure the analysis was accurate."

Erik smiled and relaxed a little.

"If you've been concerned about your mental health, don't be. Your emotions are reasonably well integrated into your personality, you have a good imagination, you relate well to others, your ego. . . ."

"What about my emotions? You said *reasonably* well integrated?"

"The tests suggest that you have some occasional problems with impulse control, especially sexual impulses."

Erik smiled.

"The indications are that you probably have an active sex life."

Erik said: "That's right. Sometimes I can't control myself. My wife complains because I want to make love too much."

"Sure, but you are still in the range of being emotionally healthy because, after all, you are a strong, good-looking, twenty-one-year-old male. Continuing on: Your ego strengths are good. We don't see an excessive use of defense mechanisms, although there are indications of a tendency to use repression."

Erik nodded.

"The Thematic Apperception Test indicates that you see older males as strongly authoritarian. Your father is probably that way."

"Yes."

"What puzzles us is that you know most of this. You are a mature person. You have pretty good self-insight. Here you are a senior starting your last term of school. You are majoring in premed, so you have a heavy class load. You are a busy, active person. Why did you volunteer to take these tests?"

"I hoped the tests would explain why I flunk physics."

"What do you mean?"

"I am taking physics for the third time now. I know all the material, but I'm afraid that, when I take the final, I'll blank out again. That repression: It happened twice. It's crazy! I know all the problems and calculations so well I am tutoring other students in the course! I have already been accepted to the university medical school, but I have to pass physics before I can start. Physics is the last requirement I have to pass, but I'm afraid I'll blank out again. Can you explain why it happens?"

"Not from the tests. Tell me, when did you first decide to go into medicine?"

A puzzled look came over Erik's face. He sat back in his chair. Moments passed. He scratched his head. Then he rubbed his neck. More moments passed. He shifted in his chair and sat staring at the ceiling for a long time. Finally, after several minutes, he shook his head and said, "I never did. I never decided to go into medicine."

"Why are you a premed major then?"

"My father always told me that when I grew up I was going to be a doctor like his brother. He said he didn't want me to spend my life driving trucks like him."

"If your father had never said anything about what you should go into, would there be another field that interests you?"

"Yes. Engineering. I would like to be an engineer."

"That's interesting. Do you see any relationship between blanking out on the physics final and your motivation for going into medicine?"

Erik smiled. "I'm starting to. Look, I've got a lot of thinking to do. I'm going to go now." He stood up and walked toward the door. Then he turned and said: "Thanks. Thank you very much."

WORK TOWARD SELF-CHOSEN GOALS

Most people understand that success is reaching a goal. What they don't understand is that self-chosen goals are much more motivating than imposed goals.

There are two essential elements in being successful. The first is having a goal. The second is reaching the goal. If a goal is self-chosen, then the motivation to reach it is much higher, and, therefore, the probabilities that the goal will be reached are much higher. If a goal is imposed, the motivation to reach it is much weaker, and the chances are much lower that it will be reached.

A lot of students' energy is spent working toward imposed goals. Required schooling, required courses, and required reading are all imposed goals. The people who impose these goals have very good intentions, but, unfortunately for many students, good intentions often do not bring desired results. And, to compound the difficulty, when students show lack of motivation, the authorities tend to react by believing something is wrong with the students. A common response from department heads is "We are having many problems because young people don't have as much desire to learn as they used to."

Goals and Motivation

It is not likely that you can stop people from attempting to impose goals on you. What you can do, however, is to spend some time thinking about what goals you would choose to work for—regardless of whether they are imposed or not. Also, if you don't see the merit in some requirement, you can take steps to find out what value it might have.

Let's say that you are taking a required course and don't see any value in it. See what happens if you talk to the instructor or someone in the field and start by admitting: "I have a motivation problem. I don't see any purpose for my having to take this course. Why is it a required course?" A person with a positive attitude will make a sincere effort to find out what the purpose of requiring this course is and will try to find some worthwhile goals to work toward.

If it happens to be an assignment within a course that you don't like, think up one that would be better and more interesting; then go talk to the instructor. Most instructors will go along with such requests.

For example:

"Dr. Bayers, I haven't been able to work up much interest in doing a paper on the topic assigned and was wondering if you would let me do the paper on another topic that does interest me?"

"What is it?"

"It has to do with these questions that I would like to find some answers to. . . ."

Whether it is in school or in a job, if you want to be more successful in life, it is a useful habit to ask, What is the purpose of this requirement? What objective is it trying to accomplish?

After you have the answers to these questions, ask, Is there some other way to do this that would be more motivating for me?

You can recognize a good, self-chosen goal by how motivating it is. If it is a goal you've picked because you *should*, then is it really a self-chosen goal? A well-chosen goal triggers energy in you.

82

Sometimes the motivational problem arises from the way the goal is to be reached. Successful people not only choose most of their goals; they also take into account the ways of working toward the goals that suit them best. People who are "internal" are more inclined to speak up and say, "I can see what has to be done, but I could do a better job if I am allowed to work in my own way."

With a little creative thinking, most difficult situations can be greatly improved.

SDP: Questioning Your Career

Students who have careers clearly in mind usually do better jobs in school than students who haven't chosen careers. Self-chosen career goals are strongly motivating.

Some students have no specific careers in mind and are in no rush to choose them. And that's fine. People should have the freedom to wait, if they choose to do so, to see what life brings their way.

For students who want information about possible careers there are many resources available. There are books and pamphlets, counselors to talk to, tests that match interests with the interests of people who are in various occupations.

What very few students do, however, even those who have selected careers, is actually to interview people presently in those careers. A practical way to obtain *realistic* information about a possible career is to arrange to have private interviews with at least three people in that line of work. Prepare for each interview by listing a number of questions that you would like to have answered. Not questions like "What do you do?" You can get that information from other sources.

We suggest questions like the following:

1. Why did you choose to go into this kind of work?
2. What do you like most about it?
3. If you could go back and start all over again would you choose the same career again?
4. What do you dislike about it?
5. What has been the most difficult thing for you to learn to deal with?
6. What could you have taken in school that would have prepared you better for this career?
7. What changes do you see taking place that a student should be preparing for?

USE FANTASIES TO INCREASE YOUR MOTIVATION TO REACH GOALS

Studies of highly successful people show that a person's fantasy life is a key determinant in his success. Psychologist David McClelland has been a leading researcher on achievement motivation for many years. He has discovered that one of the best ways to measure a person's "motivation to achieve" is to obtain a picture of his fantasy life. McClelland uses a test in which people tell imaginative stories about pictures presented to them. From this test McClelland is able accurately to predict which college students are going to be in upper management levels years later.

Four Fantasy Components Related to Motivation

The stories of highly achievement-motivated people are distinguished by four features:

1. The fictional person is working to achieve a goal, to do something better or to accomplish something that others have not.
2. He has a strong need and an emotional desire to reach the goal.
3. Reaching the goal will not be easy because of certain blocks, handicaps, or barriers, which may include lack of ability or knowledge.
4. The fictional person keeps searching for ways to reach the goal and may get some help from others, but the main reason why the goal is reached is his personal effort.

Figure 11 is McClelland's diagram of the imaginative stories of people motivated to achieve.

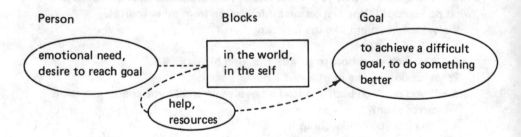

Figure 11. Four features in stories showing high-achievement motivation.

During his research, McClelland discovered that people with strong motivation to experience feelings of achievement select certain kinds of goals. These goals have a common feature. The person begins with a subjective estimate that there is about a fifty/fifty chance of reaching the goal. In tests using games, like throwing a ring over a peg or putting a golf ball into a cup, people with high achievement motivation stand at a point where, by actual count, they make about 50 percent of their shots.

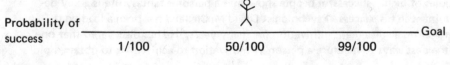

Probability of success

| 1/100 | 50/100 | 99/100 | Goal |

In comparison, people with high fear of failure, when tested on the same games, choose to stand either very close or very far away.

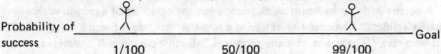

Probability of success

| 1/100 | 50/100 | 99/100 | Goal |

The person who needs to experience success picks goals for which his or her ability makes a difference. A goal that is too easy provides no special sense of accomplishment. A goal that is too difficult can be reached only with luck, and that does not create a sense of accomplishment. That's why people with achievement motivation are not gamblers. They do not become very involved in efforts whose outcomes are determined by forces beyond their control.

To gain a better understanding of how achievement motivation is developed, McClelland looked into how these people had been raised by their parents. He found that the parents had expected earlier independence, had encouraged self-initiated play activities, and had expected success. They had not over controlled or protected the children. The children had been expected to try out new things and had been praised for doing them well. McClelland describes this kind of upbringing as "independence training."

Does that mean that, if your parents have not used independence training, you are stuck with less success motivation?

Not at all. Having thoroughly studied how achievement motivation functions, McClelland experimented to see whether or not it can be taught to adults. He conducted a two-year project with businessmen in India, and his results show that it *can* be done.

His method was to have participants meet daily for several weeks to learn how to tell imaginative stories that would score high in achievement motivation. They discussed many aspects of what it means to be successful and developed some plans for themselves. They had follow-up meetings to discuss their progress and were observed over two years. At the end of that time they were more successful in all aspects of their lives (social, political, religious, and business) than were a similar group of people who had not participated in the project.

If you would like to try something of the same sort, here are some guidelines.

SDP: Increase Your Achievement Motivation

Look through several magazines, and find a picture of a person in some kind of work situation. Make up a story about what the person is thinking and feeling. Include comments about what led up to the situation she is in and what will happen in the future. Practice telling such stories until you are able to include all four success elements in every story you think up. You will gain ability to do so more quickly if you get together with several others who are interested in "success thinking" and compare your stories and scoring with theirs.

Doesn't all this attention to the possible blocks and barriers mean that, if you have achievement motivation, you have a negative attitude?

Not at all. A negative person is pessimistic about outcomes. The person who wants to achieve something is so determined to have things work out that she tries to anticipate all possible difficulties.

A person with achievement motivation is not the opposite of a person with a negative attitude. The opposite of having a negative attitude is being a naive optimist who says, "There won't be any problems." Such a person will undertake projects without pausing to think about the possibility of difficulties' arising; a successful person is both optimistic about the outcome and realistic about the difficulties involved in achieving it.

PERSONALITY AND SUCCESS

One of the better studies of the personalities of successful people has been conducted by Hal Pickle. He designed an extensive research project attempting to identify the personality characteristics of successful small-business managers. His measures of success were based on information gathered from employees, owners, customers, suppliers, creditors, bankers, and government and community sources. Then he gave each subject a series of tests designed to elicit information on the personal qualities most commonly believed to be necessary for success.

Pickle's computations relating test scores to ratings of success show that highly successful people rank highest in the following areas:

> *Characteristics and*
> *Component Traits*

Drive
　Initiative
　Persistence
　Health
Thinking ability
　Creative thinking
　Analytic thinking
Human-relations ability
　Consideration
　Cheerfulness
　Cooperation
　Tact
Communications ability
　Verbal comprehension
　Oral-communications ability
　Written-communications ability
Technical knowledge

Like McClelland's findings, Pickle's research shows how important active use of the mind is. The ability to analyze and the ability to come up with creative solutions are essential to success. This finding helps to show why we have been stressing

86

throughout this book that the key to the fully effective use of your mind is not to use it as a sponge or a tape recorder but rather to train it in the habit of asking good questions.

Notice that Pickle found that it is essential to have good human-relations ability. This finding is consistent with the results of projects carried out in a course taught by one of the authors of this book. The class was a communications course for business-administration majors. The project was to interview business people to find out what employers look for when considering hiring someone with a degree in business administration. Considering the great amount of time these students were spending taking required courses in accounting, marketing, management, and so on, it was a shock to them to discover that the first characteristic employers look for is "the ability to get along with others." Many employers said, "I can teach employees how to do the jobs I need done, but I can't teach them how to get along with others."

Does a person *have* to get along well with others? No. In fact, McClelland finds that many self-motivated achievers do not spend much energy on human relations. They tend to spend little time doing things with their families, and, if they socialize, they prefer the company of other experts.

The indications are, however, that having good friends and knowing how to develop friendships is desirable both for enjoyment of life and for success. Self-motivated achievers who aspire to high organizational positions work at being more social because they see that it is necessary for them if they are to arrive where they want to go.

Being liked, being accepted, and having friendly relations are very important. It is hard for a person who feels lonely to be fully involved in studying. That is why we insist that you should not spend too much time studying, that you should devote time to friends and other interests.

ACTUALIZE YOURSELF (BUT TAKE CARE OF OTHER NEEDS, TOO)

The Hierarchy of Needs

Every human has basic needs that, if not taken care of, can distract him from working toward goals. Abraham Maslow studied the needs people have and has contributed much to our understanding of the motivations of healthy, growing, accomplishing people. As described by Maslow, a self-actualized person

perceives reality more accurately than others and can tolerate ambiguity and
  uncertainty
is self-confident and accepts others for what they are
is problem-oriented rather than self-centered
is spontaneous in thought and action
has a need for privacy and can take a detached view of the world

87

is independent but doesn't challenge convention
has a fresh and deep appreciation for people, not a stereotyped view
has had mystic or spiritual experiences of deep personal significance
has a strong social interest and identifies with mankind
has close emotional relationships with a few people
respects all people in a democratic way
distinguishes means from ends and usually enjoys the means
has a sense of humor that is philosophical, rather than hostile
is creative
is adapted to the culture but cannot be made to conform.

Figure 12 shows Maslow's view of human needs and their interrelations. One of his more valuable insights is that our basic human needs have priorities. The lower-level needs, "deficiency" needs, take priority whenever they are activated. As each lower-level need is taken care of, new and weaker needs emerge.

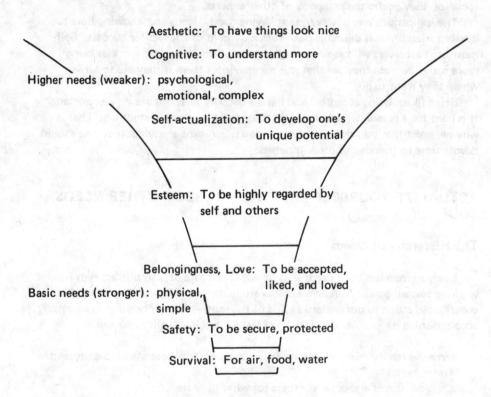

Figure 12. Maslow's hierarchy of needs.

You can read about Maslow's hierarchy of needs in almost any introductory psychology textbook. Our purpose here is to emphasize some key points in how it applies to you.

Figure 12 shows that, as you progress to each higher level, the needs are more complex and take longer to satisfy. Your need to have friends and to be accepted by others is more basic than your growth needs, but it also can be taken care of more quickly and easily than your need for esteem.

Although most people are aware of the importance of having friends, not many fully appreciate the need for esteem. Notice that esteem needs come before the need for growth and actualization, which is why it is sometimes more important to be seen with a certain person than it is to go to class; why the feelings of recognition that some students gain from causing trouble are more important than learning in school; why so much time, money, and energy go into clothes, cars, fixing up rooms, and the like; why being in certain groups and being elected to offices are so important.

According to Maslow, going beyond concern about ego needs comes when you develop a healthy *self*-esteem. High self-esteem is not present in a person who puts others down or acts superior. This person has weak self-esteem. Someone with high self-esteem doesn't have to find something wrong with others in order to look good by comparison.

The stronger your self-esteem, the less you depend upon others to take care of your need for esteem. Some students who spend almost all their time with friends do so for fear of not being liked if they leave. Because they lack self-esteem, they depend upon their friends, and they can't run the risk of being disliked.

Developing Greater Self-Esteem

How can a person gain more self-esteem?

Nathaniel Brandon has a definition of self-esteem that helps to answer this question. He says, "Self-esteem is your reputation with yourself." It takes a while to build up. You have to do things that you will like yourself for and avoid doing things that you will dislike yourself for. We should note, too, that people who brag about themselves all the time are not people with high self-esteem. They have *weak* self-esteem and are trying to reassure themselves that they are worthy of esteem.

Self-Actualization

Maslow has said that self-actualization comes from a long period of testing oneself against tough, difficult tasks; falling short; and trying over and over until a unique strength begins to emerge. True actualization is not something instilled in you by others, and it doesn't happen by itself. It occurs after you have been highly involved and working hard at something. Maslow, before his death, said that young people sitting around high on drugs or chanting mantras do not understand self-actualization. He was saddened to see so many young people waiting for actualization to strike like lightning, as if in a miraculous instant they would suddenly blossom forth into highly developed, insightful, capable people.

According to Maslow, only you can bring into existence the unique qualities that are lying dormant within you. People who have done so, who are highly self-actualized, he found, have some common characteristics. These characteristics have been listed here, but, rather than our just saying "Here they are," we suggest that you learn about them in a way that could be a growth experience for you. Find one or two individuals who have a combination of quiet inner strength, self-confidence, competence, and uniqueness. Use the interview form in Figure 13 to find out how well each agrees or disagrees that the various qualities listed by Maslow fit him.

First, ask each person to describe himself. Ask him to reveal what he likes about himself, what his strengths are, and ways in which he is better developed than others. Look for statements that suggest the presence of any of the listed traits.

Name:

Date:

Interview conditions:

Please tell me how much or how little each of the following statements applies to you:

Perceives reality more accurately than others; can tolerate ambiguity and uncertainty.

Is self-confident; accepts others for what they are.

Is problem oriented, rather than self-centered.

Is spontaneous in thought and action.

Has a need for privacy and can take a detached view of the world.

Is independent but doesn't challenge convention.

Has a fresh, deep appreciation for people, not a stereotyped view.

Has had mystic or spiritual experiences of deep personal significance.

Has a strong social interest and identifies with mankind.

Has close emotional relationships with a few people.

Respects all people in a democratic way.

Distinguishes means from ends and usually enjoys the means.

Has a sense of humor that is philosophical, rather than hostile.

Is creative.

Is adapted to the culture but cannot be made to conform.

Figure 13. Interview form.

Beyond Self-Actualization

Is there another level beyond self-actualization?

Yes and no. In his later writings, Maslow commented about the emergence of aesthetic needs (needs to have things look nice, to look at beautiful things) and cognitive needs (needs to know). These needs are weak, but, as they don't fit into the same hierarchical relations as the others, they have to be looked at separately.

Two roommates may not be self-actualized people, yet they may be in conflict because one has a strong need to have the rooms look very neat while the other is unconcerned about the rooms being messy.

SDP: How To Be Self-Actualizing

How do you rate yourself? Do you see yourself as a person who is self-actualizing?

If you wish to be developed to your fullest potential, remember that *self*-development is necessary. Select several traits or personal qualities that you would like to have. They don't have to be from the "self-actualized" list. You may, for example, realize that it would be useful to be a better listener.

Once you have selected a useful trait, design and carry out a project for acquiring it. Write out a plan of attack. Be sure to answer these questions:

1. What are the observable indications that the trait is present?
2. How will you practice acquiring these behaviors?
3. How will you measure your achievement of the goal?
4. What will the rewards be for progressing toward and achieving the goal?

IMPROVE YOUR SELF-IMAGE

Your esteem for yourself is part of your self-image. Your self-image is a collection of experiences, expectations, and predictions about what you are likely to do and what is likely to happen to you. Self-esteem influences your predictions because it affects what you believe should happen to you.

When someone is working to improve his or her self-esteem and there doesn't seem to be much improvement in his or her life, then self-image may be where the hangup is.

Self-image psychology has been an area of special interest to Maxwell Maltz, a plastic surgeon. Some of Maltz's patients came back after cosmetic facial surgery and complained that he had not done anything for them. He would show them photographs of "before" and "after." Perhaps a growth had been removed from the chin, or the nose had been reduced in size and rebuilt. The photographs showed the changes, but still the patients insisted that nothing significant had been done. Maltz was puzzled. He observed, "These 'failures' continued to feel, act, and behave *just as if* they still had an ugly face."

He says that he finally realized "that reconstruction of the physical image was

91

not the real key to changes in personality . . . it was as if the personality itself had a face." His inquiry led him eventually to conclude that "the self-image, the individual's mental and spiritual concept or picture of himself, was the real key to personality and behavior."

Wanting to help *all* his patients, Maltz devised a plan which each patient who had surgery would also have to work at changing her self-image. This system worked very well. But then the question came to him, "Since the self-image change is so important, is the surgery necessary?" He tried out his program for self-image change with a number of people who wanted surgery and found that in almost all instances the desired changes occurred without surgery! Plastic surgery was not necessary. Self-image changes had much stronger effects than physical changes.

The Importance of Visualizing

Central to Maltz's program for change in the self-image is to have each person spend time each day visualizing herself in the desired condition or situation. Visualizing things as one would like them to be has a proven effect on what happens. For example, two groups of equally matched college students were given practice in shooting baskets on the basketball court. One group practiced shooting baskets forty minutes each day. The other group spent twenty minutes practicing shooting and the other twenty minutes sitting and visualizing themselves successfully shooting the basketball through the hoop.

Three weeks later, when both groups were tested to see how well they could do, the group that had only half the practice but had spent time visualizing shot a higher percentage of baskets.

Several years ago the American ski-jump team surprised the European teams when the winter sports season opened. It did much better than anyone expected. During the summer there isn't much opportunity to jump in the United States, and it was known that the team had not practiced much. What accounted for its success? A trainer had told each jumper to spend time during the summer visualizing making successful jumps. The jumper was to go through all the feelings and sensations of the experience. First, the long climb up to the top of the hill. Then, putting on the skis. Then, adjusting the bindings, gloves, hat, and goggles. Then leaping out onto the incline, feeling the cold wind whipping the face, feeling the legs bouncing on the ice, smelling the cold mountain air, hitting the end of the ramp, and springing upward. Then soaring gracefully, keeping a good balance, hearing the quiet, looking at the landing spot far down the mountain, into a perfect landing, and then being congratulated by the crowd.

SDP: Visualizing a Successful You

Once you have chosen a goal, it can be useful to spend time visualizing yourself as having achieved it. Daydream about how people will talk to you, what certain people will say. Visualize the pleasant reactions of instructors, employers, and others you may have contact with. See yourself there—walking, speaking, feeling, and talking. Involve all your senses if you can. Imagine yourself being treated to a meal by someone who is impressed with your accomplishment.

Many school counselors see students with poor self-images who find it hard to accomplish much. They often feel lonely and unloved, not because they don't have love given to them, but because a person can experience only about as much love and friendship as he believes he is worth. He can accept only about as much credit as he believes he deserves.

Perhaps you have seen someone complimented for doing something well whose reaction is to blush and argue, "It wasn't anything," "I didn't do much," "It was nothing," "Don't thank me," "Anyone could have done that," or something similar. He is the same person who may say later, "I wish people appreciated me more" or "Why don't people ever compliment me?"

Avoid Games Losers Play

It is okay to feel sorry for yourself once in a while, but if you do it frequently you may be playing a game. A game, as explained by Eric Berne, occurs when a person follows a sequence of actions or words that manipulates others into responses that provide a hidden psychological payoff. The game is not usually fun or pleasant. The moves are superficially plausible, but the real motive is hidden. Game playing is like "conning" someone but differs in that a "con" is conscious whereas game playing usually goes on without conscious awareness.

Keep in mind that playing games is not a sign that someone is "sick." We just want to show that the games students play often have payoffs that prevent them from being successful in school. It may be that you play some games that hinder your effectiveness.

YES, BUT
A good example to start with is the game "Yes, but. . . ." It was the first game that Eric Berne analyzed, and it led to his development of transactional analysis.

"I can't seem to concentrate."

"You could study in your room instead of in the cafeteria."

"Yes, but it's too noisy there."

"Why don't you shut your door and play your radio?"

"Yes, but my roomate always talks to me."

"Why don't you. . . ."

"Yes, but. . . ."

On the surface the person seems to be asking for suggestions about how to keep from being distracted. The real purpose of the interaction, however, is to prove to others that nothing they suggest is going to work.

AIN'T IT AWFUL. . . ?
Minimartyr is walking down the hall after class and, as usual, starts a conversation by saying:

"Ain't it awful the way she loads work on us?"

". . . the way she grades?"

93

". . . how the tests are written?"

". . . how lectures are so boring?"

". . . the way we have to sit in those hard seats?"

WOODEN LEG

"How can anyone expect me to do well with the troubles I have? If you had the problems I have—my parents and I get into these big arguments on the phone each week; I have these headaches; my engagement has broken up; I lost all my notes; I can't sleep; I'm broke. . . ."

"I know someone who has lots of the same problems."

"My problems are worse! No one has problems as bad as mine."

HARRIED

Whirlwind takes on everything and volunteers for more. A moving dynamo of activity, Whirlwind works frantically on dozens of projects. On the verge of exhaustion, he charges ahead. There are meetings to attend, phone calls to make, people to see, and details to arrange. Studying? "Have to put that off until later."

Whirlwind is busy but doesn't get much accomplished. *Remember:* The more goals you have, the less likely you are to reach any of them.

STUPID

"Oh, no! There I go again. Look how dumb I am. I always do these *stupid* things. I always find some way to foul things up! I always make some dumb mistake."

True.

IF IT WEREN'T FOR HIM . . .

"I could get good grades in math if it weren't for the instructor."

"I would have a good grade average if it weren't for my counselor making me take those tough courses."

"I would go to class if the instructor weren't so boring."

"I could have qualified for a scholarship if the instructor hadn't given me a C in biology."

"I could study better if it weren't for my roommate."

These games all have predictable patterns, and they are repeated. The same thing happens again and again. The person doesn't change or find a way to deal with what happens. The gains from playing a game are worth more than whatever costs there may be—including being not successful as a student.

"If it weren't for him" is often played by students who want to justify why they aren't attending classes or studying much. These students don't want a good instructor. Their desire is to avoid classes and studying. What they want is a good excuse, a good rationalization.

There are many more games that people play, like "Alcoholic" and "Let's You and Him Fight." There are even games played by students who get top grades. By

94

mentioning a few games that the losers play, we have tried to create awareness that sometimes a person who would like to be more successful may unknowingly be acting in ways that minimize his chances of being successful.

DEVELOP "SURVIVOR" TRAITS

Maslow believed that all people have within them two strong forces: survival needs and self-actualization needs. We shall look now at an individual who takes care of both of these types at the same time, who has all the qualities we have been describing in this chapter, and who does not play games with people. We shall call him Jim Sikes. He has what is best described as a "survivor" personality.

But, before reading about Jim Sikes and "survivor" traits, pause for a moment to take this test. Check the traits that you possess, and add important other traits at the bottom of the page. Scoring will be discussed later in this chapter.

_____	sensitive	_____	tough
_____	strong	_____	gentle
_____	cowardly	_____	courageous
_____	mature	_____	childlike
_____	serious	_____	humorous
_____	friendly	_____	loner
_____	adaptable	_____	discontented
_____	self-confident	_____	self-critical
_____	dependent	_____	independent
_____	individualistic	_____	conforming
_____	lazy	_____	hard-working
_____	trusting	_____	cautious
_____	casual	_____	intense
_____	intelligent	_____	dumb
_____	involved	_____	detached
_____	leader	_____	follower
_____	impulsive	_____	thorough
_____	emotional	_____	calm
_____	creative	_____	practical
_____	shy	_____	bold
_____	proud	_____	humble
_____		_____	
_____		_____	
_____		_____	

Observer

Sikes is an observer. He is curious about the world and he likes to know what people are doing. He asks questions, and he listens a lot. He seems always to be scanning the world around him and has an awareness of what is happening.

He has a high level of empathy for people. He tries to put himself in the other person's place and to ask himself: "What is that person experiencing right now? What is it like to be him?" He accepts people for what they are and can usually find something good in everyone.

He has contacts with many groups, but he is not an active member in any of them. He avoids official positions of leadership. He prefers to remain inconspicuous and has a chameleon-like ability to be present in a group yet not be noticed. He observes groups more than he participates in them, and usually he has a good understanding of what is going on. He is likely to be consulted by the official leaders before they go ahead with plans or announce programs to their groups.

But he doesn't remain with social groups very long. He loses interest quickly. Group memberships are usually more a burden to him than a benefit.

Loner

Sikes is also a loner. Many factors account for this trait. He is a loner because he can see the solutions to problems and change his views more quickly than a group can. He has a quick understanding of situations, problems, and people. He becomes impatient waiting for a group to understand what is glaringly obvious to him, and, when he takes action, he dislikes having the success of his efforts depend upon the performance of a group or committee.

He is a loner because he has a "thing" about earning his own way in the world. He may temporarily accept help from others, but he resists letting himself fall into the habit of expecting help from others. He becomes irritated when help is forced on him. He is so determined to retain full responsibility for his survival and success that he resists anything that could undermine that responsibility. He knows, for example, about social security, medicare, welfare, and food stamps but does not consider any of them relevant to his future.

He rarely asks for help because he knows from experience that he can probably do the job better. He agrees with the saying "If you want a job done right, do it yourself."

Sikes is a loner because he needs to spend time by himself. He needs thinking time. He needs to daydream. He enjoys walking alone, waxing the car, and chopping wood. He likes physical activity that allows him to daydream while doing it.

He is a loner because of his curiosity. He needs to understand. He likes to learn how and why things work the way they do. He prefers to see things for himself. Once he finds out as much as he can, he moves on to whatever attracts him next. He rarely goes *away* from a person or group. It is more accurate to view him as losing interest and then moving *toward* something more interesting. Just as a child becomes absorbed in a toy, he gives his full attention to whatever interests him and forgets about everything else. When involved in something that interests him, he will read or work for hours at a time and be unaware of the passage of time. His powers of concentration are so strong that he may not hear people speaking to him.

Sikes is a loner because few people understand him as well as he understands

96

them. Many people, even strangers, confide in him in a way he seldom confides in others. It is rare for him to find a person to whom he can completely reveal himself. He has learned that many people cannot handle what he thinks and feels. Consequently, he has few close friends during his lifetime. He sometimes feels like a drifter who doesn't quite fit into this world, as if he were on the outside looking in.

He is deeply involved, however, and his concern for people becomes most apparent when there is trouble. He is a "foul-weather friend." He may have given the appearance of being off someplace not paying attention, but when there is trouble he shows up.

Crises

Sikes is a "crisis" person. In a crisis his strengths are revealed. He becomes extremely alert, doesn't panic or become emotional, remains calm. If anything, he is *less* emotional in a crisis than he is ordinarily. When friends are asked, "What is it you admire most about Sikes?" they answer, "He doesn't let things upset him." One of the best quarterbacks of all time, Johnny Unitas, was called Mr. Cool by his teammates. People who saw him in action said that the key to his greatness was his ability to remain calm, no matter how great the pressure.

Another survivor quality that Sikes shows in a crisis is a sense of humor. In fact, his ability to make humorous observations helps to explain how he survives. There are two principles operating here. The first is that mental and physical efficiency are directly influenced by level of emotional arousal. People are less capable of solving problems and taking complex actions when strongly aroused emotionally. Efficiency is much greater under moderate levels of arousal.

Emergencies trigger strong emotional reactions. Laughing reduces tension and arousal. The ability to laugh and joke during a crisis is thus very practical. It has a direct effect on ability to solve problems and to deal with situations efficiently. The humor showed by such fictional characters as James Bond and the surgeons in *M.A.S.H.* is not only the creation of writers' fantasies. It is typical of people with survivor personalities.

The second principle operating in Sikes' humor is that it is directed toward the immediate situation. By poking fun at a situation, he plays with it. He looks at it from all possible angles and asks: "How does this look from another point of view? What would happen if I turned this upside down? Inside out?" He keeps the situation from overwhelming him and at the same time is likely to come up with a way to survive.

When Sikes is sizing up an emergency, he waits for a certain feeling. It is the feeling that this emergency must be handled (some can be ignored), that he is able to handle it, and that he is the only person able to handle it. If all signals are "go" he swings into action.

Once he commits himself to a task, there are only two states of existence for him. Either he has succeeded, or he hasn't succeeded *yet*. He works with awesome tenacity, and he doesn't allow anyone to tell him what he cannot accomplish. He can work with sustained effort for weeks or months. When there are delays or set-backs, he doesn't make excuses or blame others. He is critical of himself when he makes a mistake, but he doesn't dwell on what might have been. He concentrates on "The next time this happens . . ." and mentally rehearses exactly how he will deal with it if he ever gets another chance.

Sikes appreciates crises because they bring out new strengths and abilities in him. He can commit himself to a task not knowing how he will handle it but know-ing that in some way he will. He is comfortable with ambiguity. He can move into unknown territories being curious about what new abilities he will develop. He de-mands more from himself than from others. He relies heavily on his stamina, crea-tivity, and ability to hold up under stress.

When a person goes through a series of stress conditions, each one stronger than the one before, he gradually acquires the ability to deal with greater and greater levels of stress. Too much all at once will overwhelm most people, but when stress is presented in gradual steps a person can learn to handle it very well. This gradual intensification is called "incremental stress."

In recent times a good example was seen when one of the space capsules headed for the moon was blown apart by exploding oxygen cylinders. The astronauts radioed back, "Houston, we've got a problem," and then proceeded to deal with the situation in a calm, capable way. Such an incident may be rated as about level-25 stress, compared with the level-5 or -6 stress that the average person encounters. The astronauts had been trained to cope with this level through incremental steps.

Sometimes, in order to survive, Sikes will adapt to a situation. He does not "ad-just," however. To adjust means to accept a bad situation and not be unhappy with it. To adapt means to tolerate an unhappy situation if it is practical to do so. A good example of the difference between adapting and adjusting has been raised by the movement toward women's equality. Many women who had *adapted* to what they experienced as bad situations decided to change things. They discovered, how-ever, that many women were not motivated to change things because they had *ad-justed* to their situations. They were not unhappy in them.

The women's movement is achieving many of its objectives because women have more inner strength than men have been willing to recognize. Men have been re-quiring women to adapt to them for a long time. The fact is that, when a rigid per-son requires others to adapt, the person who adapts is often the stronger of the two.

It is a mistake to view adaptability as a sign of weakness. Sikes, for example, may alter his behavior but not his standards or beliefs. His personal values are more important to him than the opinions of others. If people push him too far, he is capable of telling them all where to go. When necessary, he can stand up against pressure from powerful groups, friends, or loved ones.

He is highly sales resistant. If he doesn't judge for himself that something is of value, he is difficult to sell. In this respect, he shows qualities of healthy people described by Maslow: "Sales resistance, advertising resistance, propaganda resis-tance, opinion-of-other people resistance, maintenance of autonomy, suggestion resistance, imitation resistance, prestige resistance are all high in healthy people, and low in average people."

Self-Determined

Sikes is a self-determined person. He says, "No man is my master, and I am master of none." He is in control of what he does with himself. At times he will allow others to think that they are controlling him. He knows how independent he can be, so he doesn't have to prove it to anyone.

This quality of self-determination is linked with having accepted full responsibility for what happens in his career. His attitude is that his survival and success are his responsibility. They are not the responsibility of teachers, friends, classmates, advisers, administrators, relatives, or economic conditions. If he is caught off guard by something that causes a setback, he blames himself for not having anticipated what happened. He studies setbacks thoroughly to learn what he can from the experiences and to discover ways to prevent them from happening again.

Intuitive

Jim Sikes is "internal" in the way that Rotter uses the term, and he is "internal" in another way as well. He uses internal physical cues as sources of information. A slight tightening of his stomach may signal that something isn't quite right. He may notice that he is breathing fast. He recognizes that he is slightly tense or perspiring. If there is no obvious reason for these reactions, he asks himself: "Why am I reacting this way? What am I reacting to? What is causing this?"

Once alerted, he will continue in a normal manner, but part of his attention will be focused on understanding what is wrong. He scans the situation silently with his mind, his eyes, and his feelings. It may have been someone's tone of voice, a nervous gesture, or a forced laugh that alerted him. His sensitivity to these subtle cues alerts him when things aren't as they should be.

One reason why he survives is because he allows himself to be partly guided by his feelings. His actions are not entirely controlled by either his emotions or his mind. He is influenced by both. This combination helps to explain the wide range of responses available to him. He is sometimes the only person capable of doing a disagreeable job because he can do what he knows must be done, regardless of his feelings. On the other hand, regardless of how logical something may seem, he may hold off if he has a strong feeling against it. He may be having lunch with someone to talk about helping on a project. On the surface the project appears interesting. If, however, he suddenly has a strong inner feeling of "don't," he is likely to postpone the matter. Later he will look into it more deeply, to search for reasons to explain the feeling he has developed.

Incidentally, many people with survivor qualities report incidents that seem to be instances of extrasensory perception (ESP). A student nurse told of this incident:

Last spring I was sitting at the bus stop waiting for the 3:40 bus. It is the one I always take to work. The sun was shining. I sat there relaxed, enjoying it. The sun felt good. Then, I still don't know why, I stood up and walked back to stand near the wall of the store on the corner. I was bewildered because it was chilly in the shade by the store. I didn't want to be in the shade! I wanted to be in the sun, but I stood there. It was eerie. Then this car came racing around the corner. The teenage boy driving it lost control. His car skidded across the street and bounced up over the curb. He hit the bench where I had been sitting. It was eerie.

Two professors at the Newark College of Engineering have been testing for the presence of ESP in successful business executives. (Success is defined as having doubled company profits in the preceding five years.) Douglas Dean and John Mihalasky first ask the executives to write out a column of 100 digits. The executives are to try to predict numbers that will be randomly generated by a computer at a later time. Mihalasky and Dean find that successful executives score above chance levels and above executives who are less successful.

Creative

At universities conducting research on parapsychology, art students consistently show more ESP than other students. Artists, it seems, have an emotional openness and sensitivity conducive to ESP experiences. It is thus quite consistent to find that one of Sikes' survivor traits is creativity.

Most emergencies occur because unexpected things have happened. Crises develop because the usual solutions don't work, which means that survival of a crisis or an emergency requires an unusual solution. It requires something out of the ordinary, something that works. It requires creativity.

Creativity is defined as the production of an unusual idea that is useful. Sikes expects to survive unexpected difficulties. He quickly asks: "What will it take to handle this? What if I did just the opposite of what is ordinarily done? What might work here?"

The ability to come up with creative solutions, it turns out, is closely related to having been a good observer. Frank Barron, a psychologist who studies creativity, reports that creative people have a "perceptual," observing style. In contrast, people who are poorest in creativity have a "judgmental," dogmatic style. The principle is that the "perceptual" person absorbs a wide range of facts. He learns his world. He is open-minded. The dogmatic person judges situations too soon. When value judgments are made too quickly, the mind is shut to facts that contradict prejudices. Psychologists like Carl Jung, who first observed and described these perceptual and judgmental styles, describe such a person as making "premature closure." Closure keeps thinking limited, and stereotyped thinking is incompatible with creative thinking.

Opposing Traits

Sikes' creativity also comes from having opposing traits. He includes in his personality a kind of psychological counterbalancing. He can come up with unpredictable responses and solutions because his sensitivity is counterbalanced by toughness, his humor held in balance by deep seriousness. He is cowardly and courageous, mature and childlike, intelligent and dumb, friendly and distant, happy

100

and sad, hard-working and lazy, casual and intense, and so on. The more pairs of traits a person has, the more complex, adaptable, flexible, and creative he or she will be.

There are several reasons why opposing traits are related to survival. Our understanding of one comes from systems research. According to James G. Miller, former director of the Mental Health Research Institute at The University of Michigan, whenever two systems are in conflict, it is the more complex one that survives. At the human level, whenever people are in conflict, it is the person with the greatest inner complexity who will survive.

An explanation of the second comes from research conducted by psychologist T. C. Schneirla. Schneirla spent many years studying how creatures survive in a world of deadly hazards. One of his conclusions is that survival depends upon the ability to move in either of two directions. A creature must be able to move *toward* food, water, and life-sustaining conditions. It must also be able to move *away* from poisons, dangers, and life-destroying conditions. All surviving creatures can do both because they have opposing systems in their bodies. Physical movement toward or away from an object is possible because we have both flexor and extensor muscles. These groups of muscles are antagonistic: They work against each other. Different emotional states like anger and contentment are possible because the sympathetic and parasympathetic nervous systems work against each other.

In a similar manner, a person with opposing psychological traits is more likely to survive than a person without them. Having pairs of opposing traits is like having a reverse gear in an automobile. Without the ability to move backward, an automobile would soon be stuck. Similarly, an elevator is able to move up and down in a building, stopping at precise spots, because the car is counterbalanced by heavy weights.

It is the same with human beings. A person who can react in only one way is limited in what he can do. The more pairs of opposing traits you have, the better off you are.

Unique

Some people with survivor personalities do not have all the traits that Jim Sikes has, and each has some traits that he does not have. Every actualized person is a unique person, not exactly like any other. That's why no one can tell you exactly how to be successful as a person. The best anyone can do is to suggest qualities to consider developing because they are more likely to be useful.

SDP: Rate Your Survivor Traits

Start by counting the number of pairs of traits that you recognize in yourself from the list of survivor traits in this chapter. There are twenty-one pairs listed; if you have checked all of them and written in more in the spaces provided, then you have probably recognized yourself in the description. The more pairs of such traits you have, the closer you come to matching the survivor personality.

Any unchecked traits can be viewed as those to consider developing in yourself. Some are more important than others. The most essential skills are

Learning to observe without judging
Functioning without help or support from others
Dealing with crises in an effective way
Having a good sense of humor, playful rather than hostile
Being able to adapt to difficult situations
Acting on hunches or impulses at times
Finding creative solutions to problems
Being capable in unpredictable ways
Surviving and living a worthwhile life.

USE A PRACTICAL SELF-DEVELOPMENT PLAN

After Benjamin Franklin recognized how important it was "that the contrary habits must be broken and good ones acquired and established," he spent much time thinking about how he could accomplish these things. Knowing that habits occur when a person is not paying attention and that the number of actions a person can pay attention to is limited, Franklin "contrived the following method."

First, he made a long list of the virtues that various writers, speakers, and others had put forth as desirable qualities. Then he reduced the list to what seemed the most basic virtues:

Temperance	Sincerity
Silence	Justice
Order	Moderation
Resolution	Cleanliness
Frugality	Tranquillity
Industry	Chastity.

For each virtue he wrote out a short statement to clarify its meaning.

Temperance: Eat not to dullness. Drink not to elevation.
Silence: Speak not but what may benefit others or yourself. Avoid trifling conversation.

Franklin showed his list to a Quaker friend, who "kindly informed me that I was generally thought proud, that my pride showed itself frequently in conversation . . . of which he convinced me by mentioning several instances." So Franklin added to his list a thirteenth virtue:

Humility: Imitate Jesus and Socrates.

Temperance

Eat not to dullness.
Drink not to elevation.

	S	M	T	W	Th	F	S
T							
S							
O							
R							
F							
I							
S							
J							
M							
CL							
T							
CH							
H							

Figure 14. A sample page from Benjamin Franklin's notebook.

He made up a book, allowing one page to each of the virtues. He put seven columns on each page, one for each day of the week. Down the left-hand margin he put the initial letters of all thirteen virtues (see Figure 14).

His plan was "to give a week's strict attention to each of the virtues successively. Thus, in the first week my great guard was to avoid even the least offence against temperance, leaving the other virtues to their ordinary chance, marking every evening the faults of the day."

He saw his plan as similar to that by which a gardener works. The gardener does not try to pull out all the weeds from all the flower beds at once "but works on one of the beds at a time and having accomplished the first, proceeds to the second."

Franklin reasoned that, if he concentrated his entire effort on only one virtue at a time and kept at it for an entire week, then some of that effort should carry over out of habit into the next week while he was concentrating his conscious effort on the next virtue.

He checked his book nightly and placed a mark wherever he had slipped up. His goal was to go through the list over and over until, after "a number of courses,

I should be happy in viewing a clean book after thirteen weeks' daily examination." At first, he went through four courses a year, then one course a year, and later only once every several years.

Having presented many practical tips on how you can be more successful in your classes, as a student, and as a person, we remind you

Be practical; do not try to do everything suggested in this book.

If you try to do too much at once, the result will be similar to what happens when people make up long lists of New Year's resolutions. Within a few weeks the lists are entirely forgotten.

CHECKLIST FOR SUCCESS

_____ List important qualities, habits, and traits that you would like to develop in yourself.

_____ Devise a long-term plan that is realistic, not too hard or too easy, and exciting for you.

_____ (Optional) Talk over your plan with several people who know you well and whose judgment you respect.

_____ Get started!

IS ALL THIS REALLY NECESSARY?

Does a person have to do all these things to be successful?

No. This book is not about what you *have* to do. It is a book about what you *can* do if you choose. Everyone is successful to some degree. What we have presented here are ways to be more successful. What many students do not realize is that

1. Everyone has a *choice* about how successful he is
2. Being successful is under each person's *own control*
3. Real success comes from reaching *self-chosen goals.*

Can't a person be more successful without having to ask so many questions, use schedules, improve habits, self-actualize, and do so many checklists? Aren't there easier ways?

Yes, many.

Remember that "success is reaching a goal." Here is an example of a simple way to work at being more successful: If the job level you reach within an organization indicates career success, then you can be more successful by increasing your vocabulary. Studies have shown that, when people are matched in age and experience, there is a very high correlation between job level and vocabulary score.

Doesn't that mean that people with high I.Q.s have better chances of being successful?

Not especially. An I.Q. is not something you are born with. Your I.Q. is merely a test score. An I.Q. test measures how much you have learned and remembered in comparison with the performance of a certain group of people.

Anyone can improve his vocabulary. For some people it is easier, but anyone can do it. And, as the editors of *Reader's Digest* state each month on the page with the vocabulary test, "It Pays To Increase Your Word Power."

Another example of a less complicated approach to success can be found in the writings of Howard Stephenson. Toward the end of the 1930s, he wrote a book describing hundreds of people who had achieved financial success during the Depression years. His observations of these people led him to conclude that each of them had three essential qualities: imagination, nerve, and tact. Now more than eighty years old, Stephenson says that today, almost forty years later, he believes even more strongly that any person with imagination, nerve, and tact will be successful.

Notice, however, that both these examples are related to financial success. In this book we have given much attention to success as a human being, which involves a lot more. No matter what a person's job level or income, if we look at how successful he is as a human being, then we get into such questions as

How good a listener is the person?
Is he self-actualizing?
Does he develop more character, uniqueness, and inner strength each year?
How good is he at establishing and maintaining good friendships?

Friendships, as we have repeatedly said, are extremely important to success as a person. In the next chapter we shall show what leads to feelings of friendship and what you can do to build and maintain good friendships.

REFERENCES AND SUGGESTED READING

Eric Berne. *Games People Play* (New York: Grove, 1964).
D. Dean & J. Mihalasky. *Executive E.S.P.* (Englewood Cliffs, N.J.: Prentice-Hall, 1974).
Ken Ernst. *Games Students Play* (Celestial Arts, 1972).
Benjamin Franklin. *Autobiography and Other Writings*, ed. by Russel B. Nye (Boston: Houghton Mifflin, 1959).
David C. McClelland & David G. Winter. *Motivating Economic Achievement* (New York: Free Press, 1969).
Maxwell Maltz. *Psychocybernetics* (New York: Simon & Schuster, 1960).
Abraham Maslow. *Motivation and Personality* (New York: Harper, 1954).
Abraham Maslow. *Toward a Psychology of Being* (Princeton: Van Nostrand, 1968).

Hal B. Pickle. *Personality and Success* (Washington, D.C.: Government Printing Office, *Small Business Research Series No. 4*).

Harold Sherman. *How to Make ESP Work for You* (New York: Fawcett Crest, 1964).

Howard Stephenson & Joseph Keeley. *They Sold Themselves: A Practical Guide to Personal Achievement* (Hillman-Curl, 1937).

How To
Have a Few Good Friends

© 1967 United Feature Syndicate, Inc.

"Dr. James?"

"Hello, Sid. Come on in."

"Dr. James, could I ask you a question?"

"Sure, Sid, what is it?"

"In psychology class you teach us a lot about how to understand human behavior, but I can't find the answer to my question any place."

"What's that?"

"How do I keep from being so lonely?"

"Well, what have you tried?"

"I used to drive people places in my car—sort of a free taxi service—but that didn't work. I was moving and hauling stuff all over the place, but still no one was friends with me."

"What else have you tried?"

"For a while I paid for everything. Cokes, hamburgers, movie tickets, popcorn, ice cream, but that kept me broke. I tried telling jokes. I bought a joke book and each time I was going to be with people I would memorize four or five jokes to tell."

"How did that work?"

"People laughed sometimes. But sometimes I couldn't tell if they were laughing at me or at the joke. It didn't make anyone more friendly. It always ends up the same. They thank me for the ride or the ice cream or laugh at the joke, and then go off with other people. I need friends, too! How can I get people to like me?"

As with success, you have a choice about how many close friends you have. Having friends is not a matter of luck or having money or having a great personality. Feelings of friendship are created by a combination of variables that you can control.

HAVE FREQUENT CONTACT

Research into what causes feelings of friendship to develop between two people shows overwhelmingly that the main contributing factor is frequency of contact. That is partly why we have emphasized so often in this book that a realistic plan for being more successful in school should include frequent opportunities to spend time with friends.

Research in college dorms, in housing projects, and in neighborhoods shows a very consistent relationship between feelings of friendship and how often the friends have contact with each other. One study, for example, of married students assigned to apartments in housing units found that couples living in certain apartments were named as friends more frequently than would be predicted by chance. The apartments were at the foot of the stairs. Observation finally revealed that these couples were seen more frequently because the garbage cans were located near the bottom of the stairs!

Many such studies indicate that, in general, the closer you live to someone, the more likely it is that he will name you as a close friend. Once you understand how frequency of contact influences feelings of friendship, you can see why certain conditions predict that someone might have fewer close friends at school:

Living at home instead of in a dorm and not joining a fraternity or sorority
Being married to someone who is not a student
Working full time while going to school
Studying all the time
Training full time for individual athletic events like swimming and cross-country track.

Frequent contact is not enough to make someone feel friendly toward you. You know from your own experience that there are people with whom you have had frequent contact and whom you have *disliked*. Without contact, however, other important factors do not have much chance to work.

BE A GOOD LISTENER

People you have contact with will feel friendlier if you have a sincere personal interest in them and if they discover that you have attitudes and interests similar to theirs.

How do you accomplish this? Ask questions and listen with an open mind.

Dale Carnegie, author of *How To Win Friends and Influence People*, states: "You can make more friends in two months by being interested in other people than you can in two years by trying to get other people interested in you." Why should other people be interested in you if you aren't interested in them?

Everyone, in one way or another, acts according to self-interest. A major publishing company spent many thousands of dollars studying what motivates people to buy. The conclusion was "The great, fundamental principle, certainly not our discovery but profoundly confirmed by our surveys, is that to each and every reader the most engrossing and utterly fascinating subject in all the world is himself." (Marc A. Rose in *Writer's Handbook*, 1967)

Accepting versus Judging

Being a good listener requires more than just keeping your mouth shut. Good listeners have a wide range of acceptance for what they learn about others. This is why so many people feel friendly toward a person with the survivor personality. If we compare observing, open-minded people with judgmental people, the ranges of acceptance and rejection look like the following:

Open-minded

accept	neutral	reject

Judgmental

accept	neutral	reject

Notice that the open-minded person not only has a wider range of acceptance but also has a wider neutral range, in which what is learned is neither accepted nor rejected. The judgmental person, even though remaining silent, will eventually communicate through facial expressions, body language, and what is not said that he has such mental reactions as "No one should think that" or "That's sick."

If the person you are listening to has attitudes and opinions you reject, then the chances are low that you will be a good friend of his. You can still have empathy for him, however, and that is a very desirable personal quality. Henry Ford once said: "If there is any one secret of success, it lies in the ability to get the other person's point of view and see how things are from his angle as well as your own."

What about the person who doesn't try to see things from your point of view?

He is not making an effort to be friends with you. This is not a perfect world. It is an unrealistic goal to expect everyone to like and be friendly toward you. It is unrealistic because there will be some who, as soon as they detect your need to be liked by everyone, will delight in frustrating you by not liking you. Remember, no matter how hard you work at becoming what other people would like you to be, there will always be someone who is unhappy with you. That is why your opinion of yourself is the most important opinion in your life.

110

Up to this point we've seen that frequent contact sets up the opportunity for friendship, that listening helps to show that you are interested in the other person and can lead to discovery of similar interests and attitudes. Here are some suggested "do"s and "don't"s to follow during the initial stages.

SDP: Guidelines for Starting Friendships

Don't start off by trying to flatter or praise a person. Too many positive "strokes" have a reverse effect. He becomes suspicious. He is on guard, wondering "What is he selling? What is she after?"

Don't give lots of praise to everyone. Praise from a person who thinks everyone is fantastic all the time is not valued as much as a compliment from someone who gives occasional praise when it is deserved.

Do wait until a person knows that you have seen something about her worthy of interest or praise. Your praise will then be experienced as appropriate, rather than as manipulative.

Do tend to be selective in your praise. The more positive comments you dish out, the less their value.

Do express some disagreement if you can follow up later with a positive observation. When a person starts off with negative feelings about others and then shifts to positive feelings, he stimulates the strongest feelings of friendship. More, in fact, than the person who has always liked everything she's seen.

GOALS IN FRIENDSHIPS

After the first basic steps have been taken, other, more subtle factors have to be brought into play if real feelings of friendship are to emerge. Here are some observed features of good friendships. Friends have the freedom to become irritated or angry at each other. You don't feel truly close to someone who is never angry at you. In any relationship, the strong positive feelings tend to disappear if the negative ones are controlled and suppressed.

Friends feel equal to each other. Feelings of friendship cannot exist when you feel superior or inferior to someone. Friends are comfortable being seen together, letting people know they are friends.

Friends reveal their inner selves to each other. They share personal feelings and private thoughts not usually revealed to others. Their openness with each other is natural and spontaneous. They do not have to prove anything. They don't try to give false or distorted impressions of themselves to each other.

Friends accept each other as they are. They don't try to control or change each other.

Friends experience each other as unique. A friend says that no other person on earth is quite like his close friend.

Recall for a moment a point made in our discussion of attitudes. A change in attitudes can lead to a change in behavior, but the reverse is also true. A change in

111

behavior can lead to a change in attitudes. If you keep the preceding list in mind and act as if you are close friends, then strong feelings of friendship have a good chance to develop.

Manipulation

Isn't it artificial to follow a plan like this? Isn't this manipulating people to do what you want?

Everything we do influences the actions of others. It is not manipulation any more than a person manipulates others by doing the reverse. Let's say we observe a student who rarely spends time with others. He seldom says hello to others unless greeted first. He is not interested in other people, but he likes it when someone is interested in him. Other people's views turn him off. He never compliments anyone on something done well, even if he notices. He feels superior to many people and inferior to the few he admires.

Is he manipulating others? Yes—to avoid him! It is no surprise that others rarely feel friendship toward him. All human actions and feelings are the consequences of cause and effect. The person in our illustration is influencing people not to be friends with him, just as much as someone who acts in ways that influence people to be friends.

Friendship must be earned. It cannot be given. Sure, a person can feel friendly toward lots of people, maybe all people, but his feeling is a sort of "brotherly love." It is a feeling that comes from knowing that there is some good in every person and that there are some common bonds among all people. But that is different from the special, close bond of friendship that occurs with only a few people.

SDP: Guidelines for Successful Friendships

Select someone to test these principles on. Choose a person you feel equal to, someone likely to have attitudes and interests similar to yours. To increase your chances of success, select a person who doesn't seem to have many friends. Then you will be a more important person to her than you would be to someone who has lots of friends now.

Start having frequent *brief* contacts with the person. Say "Hi," wave to her as you pass, a nod and smile are best at this time. Say her name if you know it. Don't try to have a conversation for a while.

As you sense feelings of friendly recognition developing, be ready for an opportunity to ask the person one or two questions about herself. Be specific. Ask "What do you think about the new parking rules?" not "Will you tell me about yourself?"

Be willing to reveal your private attitudes or feelings *briefly*. Then quickly focus attention back on her. Don't be too quick to like her a lot. Don't lean forward listening intently, smiling, and nodding. Not at first.

Be a good listener. Listen with interest and an open mind. Try to learn what

112

it is like to be her. Try to discover what is unique about this person. As you find out what she is really like, let yourself warm up to her.

Don't be overconcerned if at first you feel that you are manipulating her or that what you are doing is so obvious she will see through it. What you are doing is acting as people who have good friends act. When a new behavior is first used, you are aware of it. Then, as you practice it and you see that it works and is okay, it gradually becomes a habit, and you become unaware of it. It becomes natural.

Concentrate less on having friends and focus more on being a good friend to others.

A Conversation
with the Authors

Note: This book was written with Tim and Al mailing chapters back and forth to each other from Providence, Rhode Island, and Portland, Oregon. After the book was completed, they got together in Michigan at the home of a mutual friend, James V. McConnell, to talk about the book. Their conversation was recorded and we have reproduced it here because of the perspective it gives to the *Student Success* book and because it shows how two "C" average students went on to obtain Ph.D.'s.

Al: Tim, I've been waiting for months to ask you this question.

Tim: What?

Al: I've been reading all these chapters you've written about generating questions, using charts, schedules, checklists, and so forth, and I want to know, *truthfully now*, did you do all this when you were in school?

Tim: No, I didn't. I have to admit I did *not* do all this when I was in school. When I was in school, the first two years of my undergraduate existence I would read and reread and reread all the chapters. . . . I would read over my notes again and again and I would periodically try to figure out from the books what questions might be on the tests. Basically, I was a really lousy student. I probably spent roughly two or three times too much time studying.

Al: What changed all that?

Tim: When I got into my junior year, I started taking a lot of courses where we knew the instructors gave the same tests year after year. So I went about getting old tests and I found out that when I practiced answering all the questions out of them that I did very well in the courses. My grade point went up. It went up from about a C+ average when I was in the first two years. My junior year I had brought it up to close to a B average. By my senior year, it was better than a B average. In my late junior and senior year I spent probably a third of the amount of time studying that I used to spend because I finally realized most of the courses required just answering questions that I could predict from a variety of sources of information. Graduate school became even more of that because I started working at the University Reading Service and I taught a lot of courses in reading improvement there. I taught people of different age ranges, began using these techniques in my own graduate courses, and worked with a lot of students who were having problems. So, to answer your question, I didn't at first. I was a lousy student. I spent far too much time studying, was very, very unhappy, considered dropping out of school several times, hardly dated at all my first two years, and spent a lot of time going over the same information time and time again. It became a very dull and boring existence and I was very displeased with school.

Al: That was my experience very much, too. At the end of my sophomore year, I had a GPA of about 2.1. I saw the other students were getting more out of school than I was...

Tim: Yeah, Yeah.

Al: ...so I joined the service. I went in for three years in order to try to figure out what I wanted to do with my life and what I wanted to get out of my schooling, just to grow up a little bit. So, after three years, I went back to school and gradually began to learn ways of getting better grades. It was a slow process. I've been thinking back to the things that influenced me and one of the key things came right when I was a junior and I first started back in at school. I went to talk to my psych professor about why I didn't seem to be doing well at school and why studying was hard and all that. And he said, "You ought to accept the fact that studying can be hard work. To some of us it can be just as hard as physical labor. Once you face up to that reality, then it's not so difficult to deal with. Studying isn't always fun." I approached it more like, occasionally I had to do some hard work, and it was a lot easier. In fact, I got a 4.0 the next semester.

Tim: It's very interesting how many people just sort of say, "Forget it, I'm gonna quit." They go off to do something else, like work in a garage or travel to the southwest or whatever it might be because they think, "When I come back, I'll be more mature and I'll be ready to study." I found with myself, I remember in my sophomore year I took a trip to another college down south where I thought it would be easier than the University of Michigan, which is a real break-neck sort of school. I found they required you to do the same type of work under the same types of conditions. It was just that no school was that much different from any other. Maybe different calibers of students were in different schools, but the schools were basically the same. They are all tough. The community college in my home town was probably tougher than where I was going to school.

115

TIM SAYS:

A good study area should be free of distractions.

When predicting exam
questions, two heads are
usually better than one.

Close friends say that no other
person on earth is quite like
their friend.

AL RECOMMENDS:

A flexible study schedule is best in case friends interrupt . . .

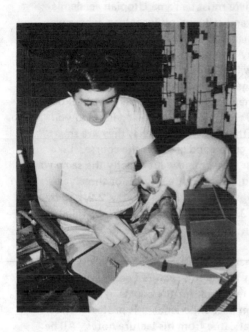

. . . or you may have to help a friend
fix something.

You should have time for
doing what you want with friends.

Al: Yeah, I found that also. I taught some psych classes in nursing schools and what happens is that a number of high school graduates choose to go into nursing because they feel that they don't want to get into the academic grind of the university. And what they discover in nursing school is even a *tougher* studying situation. They have to master chemistry and physiology and neurology and anatomy and diseases and medicines. . . pharmacology. They do laboratory work and for many of them it's just so overwhelming that they actually would have had it easier, as far as studying goes, if they had gone to the university.

Tim: That's quite true. I came back after this trip and I said, "Well, what it amounts to is I've got to become a better student. I have got to quit making up excuses about how teachers don't like me, or how this school's designed to get rid of the students or hurt people and all that. All of these soft feeling philosophies about how people are out to get you. The paranoid dilemma a lot of students get into about, "Well, because they are not handing me these grades on a silver platter and making me work, there must be some Utopian academic community where we just sit around and talk and philosophize, where we are graded on our intentions rather than our product.' "

Al: There are some students who will play that game. There are some bright students. I've seen that where they will go around acting like they never study at all and they're always playing bridge, sitting out in the sunshine reading a paperback book or having coffee someplace, out on their bikes or backpacking perhaps. And then they come in and they get an A in the course and you wonder how in the heck did they do that. Part of it is that they are smart enough to figure out what it takes to get a good grade in the course. Like you mentioned about picking up your GPA, mine went exactly the same way. I had a 2.1 in my sophomore year and I went in the service for three years. Then I came back. By the end of my junior year I had about a 2.9, and by the time I graduated it was well over 3.0. In fact, like you said, learning to predict questions on the exam?

Tim: Yes.

Al: I had one class I took in my senior year, by that time I knew this psych prof well and how his mind worked. I was taking this required course, a two-hour required course, and I purchased the textbook for the course, glanced through it to see what it was like. I knew from past experience this professor never asked questions on the final exam that came from his lecture notes. All he asked were questions from the textbook and I knew the kind of question he asked. So I did not do any studying all year long until final exam week. I finished a final in the morning, went back and had lunch and then I had two hours from the end of lunch until my final for this particular course. And in two hours I went through the book, memorized what I knew he would ask on the test, went in, took the final, got an A on the test, got an A in the course, and to this day I have no idea what that course was or what the textbook was! But it was a challenge. I was kind of testing out my philosophy, my knowledge. But I used that time in more productive ways. I really didn't care about that

118

course. I needed the hours for my major so I used my time to do other things I really enjoyed more.

Tim: Now and then you find that a course is not all that valuable but you have to take it. It is, in your estimation, a waste of time! This is where these techniques stand out most to me. You've really got to figure out what the instructor wants and give it to him with the least strain on your part.

Al: Did you always attend classes? I always did; I never cut classes.

Tim: No, never. I was very fearful of the consequences. I don't see that in students today like I used to see it.

Al: And when I'm teaching now, actually if a student is unhappy about being in a course . . . and let's say it's a required introductory class . . . I would just as soon have them stay away. So myself, I don't care if they cut. Although I do hold them responsible for whatever is presented in the classroom and they are going to be tested on that.

Tim: Exactly . . . . One of the things I don't want students to feel, is that we are just trying to teach them how to get good grades. To me grades mean very little. I'm really concerned about what you can do after you get out of the class. I have been convinced by seeing results of people studying this way that they have more time to do things that they want, they have a better comprehension of what they really want to know and they have done it under a much more rewarding system because there's such great predictability that if you study in this way, you will learn the answers to questions which you think are important and somebody else thinks they are important. And you still have time to go off in other directions that your instructor doesn't think are so important, but you think are important.

Al: I think, Tim, that is why you and I have gotten along so well in writing this book. I believe very much the same thing. What we are aiming at is teaching a person how to be in better control of her own education, and we are setting it up in a way that there is also the correlated advantage of being able to get better grades in classes. But the key thing is managing your own education. I do some workshops in personal growth and self-development and things like that, and one of the central points I try to drive home is that the key to self-actualization is learning how to ask good questions.

Tim: Right.

Al: Because only you can discover your own potential. To do that it takes asking questions. Questions are the path to the unknown. That's the route. So this thing of teaching the person how to develop himself more quickly and be in charge of that by asking questions all fits.

Tim: I have another goal, too, and I guess that's the sort of thing that parents run into with their children. You know, you always have your parents telling you, "Well, do it this way, because I learned the hard way and the way you're going is not the way to go." And you seldom believe it. You say, "I'll go my way, because I think it's right" and then later on you may say, "I wish I'd done what my parents told me." Time and time again in my own experiences, I've gone through this very painful process of not sitting down and

119

asking these questions before I take each course or each time before I study for a course. What do I want to get out of this time in my life? What will I be able to do after this period of time? What questions will I be able to answer?, etc. Many students just go to a class and say, "Well, this is going to be another hour of time that I pass towards getting my degree." If that's the case, to me, time is all you have and you're just wasting it.

Al: Yes, that fits. That's why I included that section about attitudes. That was pretty much my approach. If I was sitting in a required course, I assumed immediately that there had to be a very good reason why a lot of people running the educational system decided that this particular topic was of such importance they were going to *require* that each student go through it. They wouldn't even make it an elective opportunity. So, if it was required, I figured that that was a vote of confidence for the course rather than a hassle of some kind.

Tim: I would like to save a lot of the students who read this book, all the time that is wasted, when they go around and say, "I really hate going to school." You know there are so many good things to do in college and the fact is, that you could spend your time doing them and not going to class and possibly be better off. And I knew a lot of guys who did that, who came to school and said, "Look, there are a lot of other things at this college which are considered intramural activities or pastimes you can take part in when you are not studying. In fact, I think they are more beneficial things for me to be doing, such as belonging to organizations, or clubs, or activities or whatever it might be." I'm not saying they were right or wrong, but, by gosh, they did learn to get as much out of their courses as they could as quickly as possible so that they could go on to do more important things for themselves. If that is what you want to choose as your goal in college, *fine*, but don't be hollering and screaming about how you would like to be able to do those things but you can't because you have to spend all your time studying. I know how to help people study. We have told them how and if they do it, they'll be a lot better off.

Al: What about this other thing of peer group pressures? There are certain norms, and it's stronger at some schools than others and certain groups within schools, to not get good grades. For example, I was reading in *Time* magazine recently about one of these English members of Parliament who was in trouble and they gave a brief background of his career, military record, and his schooling. It said, "He got gentlemen's grades at Cambridge," which means that, at one time if you were a gentleman and you went to Cambridge, the tradition was to not try to get top grades, but to get a C average. That is what a "gentleman" got because there were other more important things than just studying to get grades. Sometimes they say at school "Get the Gentlemen's C in the course." Your peer group will put pressure on you if you get an A in the course, like you are not quite one of the group if you get that kind of grade. That can be a tough thing for some students to deal with. Sometimes it operates on a person without the person realizing it. They just figure this is the way it is.

Tim: I haven't seen a lot of that. What I have seen is more with required courses where students just go in there and pass, especially in pass/fail courses. They just want to learn enough to get by. If you break your neck in a pass/fail course some people would say that's stupid. Why break your neck? Just get enough to pass the course. You have to get by that whole grade thing, and that's what I would like to emphasize. You do have to get good grades if you want to go certain places beyond college. I'm not so sure people look at your grade point averages in most businesses. They look at . . . "Do you get along with others? What are your human relations? How do . . . "

Al: Yeah! Let me break in. I have never run across an employer who asked for a grade point average. With the exception of the telephone company. The Telephone Company tends to hire managers according to GPA. But with more employers it is just the matter of . . . "What school did you go to? What was your major?" They don't ask what your GPA was. Myself, part of my problem when going to school, especially during the first three years, was that I did not realize that there was a difference between learning what interested you . . . that that was different than learning to pass the course with a good grade. Because I felt if I was learning something interesting and that I was growing as a person, then that would give me a good grade in the course. But it didn't work that way.

Tim: No.

Al: I kept getting average grades and somehow falling short. It took me a long time to realize I needed to do two kinds of learning: one was the learning just to satisfy my curiosity, and second was the kind of learning that it took to get a better grade in the course.

Tim: That is a crucial discrimination.

Al: My attitude was pretty much that when I got out in the real world on my own someplace and had a job, what was going to count was what kind of learning I had inside my head . . .

Tim: Exactly.

Al: . . . not how well I did in a course.

Tim: But very few students come to realize that. Most students are just interested in passing courses. I almost throw up every time I see students taking all kinds of pills and things like that to stay awake. When they are all through with the course and walk out in the hall, they say, "Boy, I hope I never see that book again. I am just so tired of this course." They seem to have this attitude of wanting to just get it over with. Why go to school if you just want to get it over with?

Al: I think that might be partly society's problem. The norm is that if you are a healthy person you graduate from high school and you go to college. Many students are not there for any inner feeling or any desire to learn very much at all. Some from curiosity, sure, but not a strong motivation to learn. They're there because it was programmed into them. To me it's understandable why people feel that way.

Tim: There are just some really lousy courses that people have to take. I'll admit that there are some courses that people have to take that are boring, and poorly taught, and all of that. But you've got to take them, and the thing to do is to learn to take them to get the most rewarding and least pain out of them. It's like every job. Every job is going to have its good days and its bad days. It had good parts and bad parts. There's little I hate more than a person who is going through his job during the day and he's yelling and screaming about . . . "This is such a painful task" . . . "I can't wait until the day is over." It just makes it a pain for everyone who works around him. It's really a pleasure to see people going through some hard work, which may not be the best part of the day for them, but they go through it cheerfully and make it not all that bad. They have learned to do it with a positive outlook. They say that "there is a reward at the end of this for me." I went through with friends a lot of courses we didn't want to take. They were very tough courses, and not that intellectually stimulating, but we had to take them. We did it with a lot of comraderie. Because we did it together, we made sure that we all did well. I like the idea of studying in groups because sometimes the best time to get a group of people together is when you've got an especially tough course. You really need that stimulation from one another. You say, "Hey, you're going to make it. You're doing well." Math courses were always that way for me. I really needed extra stimulation from other people.

Al: You are right. This goes along with being a better student. I found that, especially my senior year. I made sure I always got into these last minute question-answer groups before the final exams.

Tim: Right.

Al: It gets so that after awhile, when you get used to taking tests and you start getting yourself organized, you start relaxing a little bit more. You know there is always going to be another test next week. They are just going to keep coming.

Tim: Right.

Al: So you just relax and you do the best you can at each one. The question-and-answer sessions really were extremely useful to me.

Tim: It sure takes care of your ulcers and colon, I'll tell you that. You don't get all hepped up and you don't get all nervous because you don't say, "Oh, gosh, what's gonna be on that test. I'm sort of worried about it. I just can't stand thinking about that test." Instead, you say, "Hey! I think I know what is going to be on that test and I'm not all that worried. This is what is going to have to be done. I'm gonna know this information. I'm going to take it and go on to the next one." Otherwise, college just becomes a day-by-day escape from something worse. Each day you are trying to escape from knowing that you are going to have to go on to something worse the next day. Test after test after test isn't a ball.

Al: When you were an undergraduate, did you expect to go to graduate school?

Tim: I thought I probably would, but I didn't know how I would pull if off after my first two years of college!

Al: Right!

Tim: Those were really trouble. I had very little confidence. Let me tell you a
little story about how I picked up on a lot of the study skills stuff before I
got it from working at the Reading Improvement Service. I had a friend
whose name was Bill. He was in psychology and was a topnotch student.
He was a Phi Beta Kappa when he was an undergraduate and he had gone
on to Michigan's Ph.D. program in psychology. He was a guy who would
come around my fraternity house all the time. You never saw this guy with
a book during the night. He was always up in the fraternity going from room
to room talking to the guys and getting guys to go to shows, and out having
fun times. The rest of us were just breaking our necks. It was unbelievable.
I said, "Bill, how do you do it? You're Phi Beta Kappa!" He said, "I just
learned to study effectively." He was sort of one of these nonchalant guys.
He didn't say he didn't study. He just said, "I learned how to study effectively." So I was over at his place one Friday night. I came over there to
study because I couldn't study at the fraternity house on a Friday night.
He had a set of rooms at his place and he was letting me use one. He was
going out on a date, and I said, "Bill, do you have five minutes?" and he
said, "Sure." I said, "Tell me, how do you study?" He said, "What I do,
Tim, is that I walk around the room and I talk to myself as though I was
talking to a professor and the other students about the answers to important
questions. I talk to myself about what is going to be on tests. And then I
go check my books and see how my answers are." So he says, "I spend most
of the early part of the day, maybe from 11 a.m. to 3 p.m. during the day
just going back and forth over questions and answers, talking to myself. I'll
go spend time with other guys who I know who are in the same courses and
I sit and I talk to them about these things." "Well, then," I said, "you do
study a lot." He said, "I do study a lot. When I read books, I look for the
questions and answers I think are important in my area of study and then I
go talk to people at the labs and places like that. I go sit down with the
professors and talk to them about these things. They always think I am an
interesting fellow because I come and ask them important questions." Those
weren't his exact words but in essence that was what he was saying. I thought,
"If he can do that, I can do it, too." So I started practicing doing that. I
started walking around the room, talking to myself and writing questions
and answers. I modeled after a very, very effective student. And then I
would start going out at night and having a good time and drinking with the
guys and going to movies and having more dates. I was a very good student
because I saw an effective model. Prior to that he took me aside and said,
"Tim, you are paranoid. You always talk to me about how you think you
will do well in this course if the instructor likes you or if he doesn't ask
questions you hadn't predicted he would give you." He said, "You got this
paranoid dilemma about whether you are gonna make it through college
because of the grace of God. You are one of these great externalizers. You
think all these external forces are controlling you." He said, "That's nonsense.
What's controlling you, what *should* control you, is you. You should sit

123

down and say, 'What do I have to do to make it in this course,' and you should practice doing that. You should forget about the personality of the instructor; you should forget whether the class is boring; you should forget about what sort of books they are using; forget about all that because you have no control over it." And I said, "Say, thanks a lot, Bill, that's really neat of you." It turned out he went on to get a Ph.D., I got a Ph.D., and now we are both in the same area. I think that is most amusing. But it was a funny thing. They used to come up to him at the fraternity house and say, "Bill, how do you do it?" He never told anybody but me. But that got him in trouble when he was in graduate school, and I will tell you why. You are supposed to play a game when you are a Ph.D. student. You are always supposed to be there playing up to the professors, I found, at least at the school I went to. You had to be there conning the professors, at least a lot of them in certain Ph.D. programs did that. They spent a lot of time making it look like they were working, even though they weren't doing anything. Whereas Bill never did that. He went off and did his work and also had fun. They didn't like the idea that he was having fun, so they gave him a lot of trouble. They said, "You are not doing a lot of things our graduate students are doing. We don't see you at the library every night, and we don't see you doing this and we don't see you doing that." He said, "Look, man, I have published more articles than other graduate students do; I get better grades. What is the gripe?" The point is that he wasn't playing the role they expected of him. There is a part about humility in this type of thing. You have to learn to be humble.

Al: Or give the impression of working hard. I had a guy who wanted me to teach some public seminars that he was going to promote. He had a lot of experience promoting and managing rock groups. He attended my seminars and when we were talking about how to improve my presentation, he said there is one thing I should do that he felt was necessary. He said, "You are smart; you know your stuff but you make it look too easy. The key to success of any rock group is that they work hard. If they show up and play their instruments and sing their songs and do it with a minimum amount of energy, people don't feel that they have gotten their money's worth." He said, "If you pay your $3 or $4 or $10 and they exhaust themselves on stage, screaming and yelling and moving and perspiring, you feel like you have gotten your money's worth." I've seen this principle in a number of different ways since he pointed it out to me. Many times people are skillful and they are accomplishing certain things, but it doesn't look like they are working very hard. The viewer tends to feel that if they are not working hard, they don't really deserve the rewards they are getting. It is the "work ethic" that is engrained in us to a certain extent. I was watching a television show on circus performers and I suddenly realized when you watch one of these guys on the high wire there is usually some spot in their act where they start bouncing the wire back and forth as if they are almost going to fall off. This is just show business. Most of these high wire performers are so good they could walk across that

124

wire relaxed, with no false movements and no close calls of any kind. But what they do is add that to the act because the audience feels that it is so dangerous. For their money they almost saw this guy get killed. Through good coordination and effort he survived that tough moment, and he made it through, and they give him a huge round of applause and believe he is one of the greatest they have ever seen . . . . because he added in that extra thing of almost falling. He is so good he really didn't have to do that.

Tim: That's right!

Al: I touched on this a little bit on one part of the book of suggesting to students, if they have a chance, that they look through lots of papers that students turn in and look for that element of hard work that shows through. If I get a paper that is half a page long and it looks like it took about twenty minutes to write, that student is not going to get an A for that paper. The students who get A's for the paper are the ones that have obviously put some time and effort into it. They asked questions; they did a little inquiry to find out what the answers were; they have gotten involved in this. There is an expenditure of energy that shows through in the papers that they have turned in. Usually I have to feel that before I feel comfortable at all in giving a student an A. It is not enough to jot down a few words.

Tim: You know, students learn that game quickly, sometimes to their detriment. I have a series of questions which I ask the students to answer after they read each of the 20 chapters in a book. I had a number of students who actually wrote down the questions; not only the answers but they wrote down the questions, too. It took twice as much writing. I said to them, "Why did you do that?" And they said, "I just wanted to show you that I was really interested." I replied, "You are just wasting hours of time doing that." I think it is that thing we were talking about before. Students sometimes think they are studying and doing well if they are putting in their time. If they are expending their energy and putting in their time they say, "Dammit, I am working and working hard and will get a good grade." And then when they get those lousy grades back, they say, "That no-good!"

Al: I worked hard.

Tim: I worked hard and I really got a rotten deal.

Al: Sure. I had something like that happen once when I was a Teaching Fellow. I started off the course and asked the students to do reading notes they were to turn in. This was the first set of reading notes, and most students' ranged from one to three pages. I had one student who turned in 150 pages of reading notes. Now, this is after the first two weeks of classes! There is no way she was going to cover five books and have done that much in the way of reading notes. So I rejected it, and I said, "This is much too much. What's going on here?" As I talked to her, I found out she was a transfer student, and the impression I got was that she had a lot of her old term papers from her previous classes and she just put them together and handed them in. She was going to turn in so much that there would be no way I couldn't give her an A grade. But I didn't. I said, "I don't accept this, because this doesn't show what I wanted. It is more like a bunch of term papers." And her immediate reaction was . . . "You are out to get me. Why are you out to get me? Because this is O.K." In her mind, she had decided that this satisfied the requirement. She admitted the reading was done at her previous school, but she wouldn't listen to me when I said that book reports weren't the assignment. I started to get suspicious about her character. I took her paper and looked up the books she was supposedly citing and quoting and found out that these papers she turned in were highly plagiarized. I don't know what happened to get her out of the previous school, but it was obvious that there was something pretty phony going on. She got so wild about it, I had to turn it over to the Dean of Students. She was not only trying to con me with her 150 pages of reading notes, but what she turned in was not original. It was plagiarized. Yet she really believed that I hated her; I was out to get her; I was like all the other instructors at the other schools who had decided that she was not going to make it through college. Man, I really had a case on my hands.

Tim: Sometimes I don't fault a person like that because they don't really know. They never had somebody say to them, "Look, sweetheart, if you do this you are going to make it. Do these things; study effectively by doing these things. You won't have to do all that other garbage. It is like people you run into who like to make the super great impression the first time. Recently I ran into a guy who said, "I am Joe Dokes, a nice guy." I almost threw up. I have had several people do that to me. There is some big thing going around lately about saying, "Sam Jones, a nice guy," or "A friendly fellow," or "a guy you would like to see more often." I think, "Why are you trying to make the big first impression on me?" It is superstitious and meaningless behavior which they think will get them somewhere.

Al: I have not had enough nerve to do it, but along the line of not being too friendly at first if you want friends, I have thought several times of walking up when I first meet somebody and say, "Hello, I am not going to say that I am pleased to meet you, because you will probably be as biased and narrow a human as most people."

Tim: And people won't buy the book if you say that! And that last story about that girl. If a student read that, she would say, "He's unfair. She did a lot of hard work, didn't she? She did 150 pages for Dr. Siebert and he flunked her." Some people would really be mad. But I agree with you; that happens in all schools. There are certain students we all know are con artists. They come and they try to spend most of their time with you talking, just spending time with you and trying to convince you what nice guys they are. I am tempted to say, "Look, man; it's not that I don't like you, but I got 350 other students." They figure the way to get a grade is to be your friend.

Al: That is their approach. Unfortunately, with a few professors, it works.

Tim: It really does. I've seen instructors spend hours of their time with one or two students and give the students higher grades than they've earned.

Al: Did you ever play up to profs?

Tim: Never. I avoided talking to them . . . until my senior year when I started asking questions I wanted answers to.

Al: I wouldn't talk to profs. I'd get nervous. It wasn't until graduate school that I called a prof by his first name, and that was because he ordered me to. In my case, becoming a better student, I see a series of things that happened. One was self-image. Once I became aware of this, then I could look back at a specific example of how self-image made me get low grades my first two years. I went to college when a number of the kids I ran around in high school with went to the same college. There was this one guy I really looked up to. He was a "big man on campus." He was very mature, could date almost any girl that he chose to be interested in.

Tim: Suave . . . .

Al: He was so suave. He could talk on a friendly basis to professors and not be embarrassed like me or nervous. We were taking a freshman chemistry course. He was pre-med and I was pre-med. I listened to the professor and I read the first chapter in my chemistry book. The professor announced he would have a weekly quiz each Friday. So I took the first weekly quiz and I got 100%. My idol, the intelligent, sophisticated, suave, capable, mature person got 85%. It shocked me that he got 85% and I got 100%. So the next week we took the weekly quiz again. That time I didn't read my chemistry book as much. He got 89% or something close and I got 90%. I *still* beat him! It took me about three or four weeks before I was able to consistently get a score of 70% on the weekly quizzes, which seemed to me to be appropriate, considering that this guy's level was about 85–90%. And considering my relationship to him, it did seem reasonable. I am not saying there was a lot of conscious thought going on, but looking back, I can see that each time I got a better grade than he did, I stopped studying so hard. I stopped preparing for the test; I stopped taking such good notes in the class. I just started acting in ways that led to my getting a grade that fit my self-image as measured against him.

Tim: I used to see that with a lot of guys; with the athletes around school. If you went to class, you had your jacket on and just sat there and listened and chatted with the girls and things like that; made coffee dates; took a few notes. At the end, you would try to get some old tests or things like that and you try to make it through. There is that image that some guys live up to. It seems that one of the key things to getting good grades is to not have a loser's image. It's to say to yourself and say, "I'm not too personally concerned with how I look to this professor, or how I look to others. I am concerned about how I look to myself. What do I really want to be able to do here, independent of what others think of me?" Then you set those goals up for yourself. You say, "I want to get good grades here. And I'll spend so much time doing that. Now, if my friends happen to go along with this, that's great; if they don't, maybe I need new friends."

Al: To me that's a second or third step. The first step, it seems to me, is just to spend a little time fantasizing about what would it be like if I got a good grade and you go through, mentally, all the important people; the person you are dating, your roommate, people in the dorm, friends you graduated from high school with, parents, teachers back at high school. And just think, what if I got an A in this course and so on and so forth. What if my mother found out; my sister found out; if my date found out I was getting A's. A lot of kids can't handle that. They *cannot* handle it if someone found out they were getting A's, because it just doesn't fit with what other people perceive them as. And so they act in ways consistent with other people's perceptions that they are very mediocre.

Tim: That's true. When you find yourself acting in ways which are different from those people's perceptions of what you should be, sometimes you catch a lot of flack for it. But if students act in those ways and change their performance, they become better students, and a lot of their old friends fall by the wayside. Not that this is a bad thing either. It is just that their interests change, they go into different things, and their friends' interests change and they go into different things. Naturally that happens as a person changes throughout life. You often feel bad about this and you say, "Hey, I don't see so and so anymore." But when you think about it, it may be because you are a new and different person. Your interests and your goals may be totally different from those of your old friends. Then you go back to the tenth year or twentieth year high school reunion and you say, "Isn't this strange?"

Al: Relating to what I was saying about acting in ways consistent with what other people expect, this is exactly what women have been struggling with for a long time. And many women, to be "nice" people, kept themselves fairly weak, subservient in a way that would not threaten the male ego or the male status because the man could not handle it. It's like saying, "I love you, and because I love you, I will help you avoid experiencing distress or nervousness. If I were to be strong, you would feel that way; so to keep you from being upset, I will keep myself weak." And there are a lot of people who make that choice.

Tim: I think what we are saying to the student is, "Look, you've got a choice."

Al: Most people don't realize it is a choice.

Tim: I said that to myself when I was going to drop out of college. I said, "You've got a choice. You can either go back there, and gut it out and figure out how to do it more efficiently and effectively, or you can quit. But if you quit, what is going to happen to you?" So you go back and you find out— Hey! There are some very, very simple ways of improving the means by which you get through school. And once you do that, you have a lot more fun in life. I am not saying there is any great sort of extraspecial experience. It is just a matter of: Hey! You do this and this is what happens. You can't beat that.

Al: What does our book accomplish that other books don't?

Tim: I think it compiles and condenses probably the most effective set of study techniques from many of the various learning and study skill centers. In preparing the book, I spent a considerable amount of time just looking over what everybody else had done. And I concluded several things. One, almost every book was far too large and asked people to do things which, in fact, were really very questionable procedures. In essence, we are suggesting those things which are most effective in helping students become more successful. I didn't include anything that I didn't use with a large number of students and which wasn't recommended by a lot of other well-known people in the field.

Al: We certainly have an unusual combination here, with your strong emphasis on the behavioral approach and my focus of attention toward introspection, self-examination, visualization, self-image, self-development, and such. I'm pleasantly amazed at how well our approaches have meshed. I think I know why, though; because I use descriptive rather than hypothetical constructs.

Tim: Whatever you did, yours is the first description of self-actualization that has made sense to me. Everything else I've read is unintelligible.

Al: We certainly have an interesting combination. One thing I would say is that we have written a book that I wish I had had when I was first starting college.

Tim: Many students who have talked to me about prepublication copies of things that are in this book have said things such as, "Hey, that's really good. I wish I could have had that when I was a freshman in high school or a freshman in college. Can I have a copy of this?" or "Can I Xerox a copy of this to give to my brother who is starting college?"—or to my nephew or my son. They really like it because it is in layman's terms. Things are easy to understand; not a lot of psychological mumbo jumbo which they couldn't go out and apply.

Al: And having put together a lot of practical tips, we don't say that they have to do it. It's, "Here is what you might find will work for you if you choose to want to be a better student, and these are things that other students and we have been able to make work. Give it a shot and see if it works for you."

Tim: Every one of the things that I have suggested in this book I have used with large numbers of students. I started using these techniques in 1968. I have had all types of students with a variety of problems. One of the things I really think is interesting about what we have done is the fact that, when I ran into these students, a large number of them were having psychological problems, *supposedly*. They were having self-image problems, self-esteem problems, low ego, however psychologists want to classify them. The main thing that makes students feel better is doing better in their classes. It's like psychologists want to give everybody therapy, give them special counseling, give them special this, give them special that, and they overlook the key problem. That is, you can't feel good about yourself in school and college unless you can do well in class. It sure helps your self-esteem if you can go to class and answer questions and ask good questions and feel good about yourself in the majority of your working day. I don't care how much money you pay most people, they are not going to stay in jobs long unless they like what they are doing. I believe that from personal experience. Students will come to me and say, "Everything is terrible," and I say, "How are your

129

grades going? How is school going?" And the student says, "That's the main problem. So I say, "Let's focus on that." And then they say, "But . . . I am having a problem with my girl . . . my parents are doing this . . . " I say, "I am a study skills counselor. I am going to help you get better grades; help you read better; help you do all these things students should do better. Let's work on one thing at a time. If you feel you've got problems in other areas, go to the counseling center." That's one of the problems I see in colleges, especially in counseling centers. They are trying to help students solve academic problems by working on social problems. Very few schools have real true academic improvement centers. Or they may have a small reading improvement program, but seldom do you get somebody who can help you learn to write better and to study better and all of those things.

Al: In the Student Counseling Center, oftentimes you get a psychologist . . .

Tim: Maybe a social worker.

Al: . . . or other persons there. They are the counselor types, and they accept the definition of the problem because it is what they were trained to do. Because a kid keeps having a problem with girls or boys or whatever. So they figure if they can get this personality shaped up, maybe the grades will improve.

Tim: But the students still don't know how to study. We used to have graduate students come in and say, "My parents spent all this money, I spent all this money, I work all the time, and I am not making it through school." We'd test them and they'd have a sixth or seventh or eighth grade reading level. Then, they'd probably have medical textbooks that they read and reread. You can't do that, keep rereading a medical textbook. Students are doing what I consider punishing and injurious psychological behaviors. They are involved in a behavior which has no payoff towards the goal they are trying to accomplish. It is a really very painful thing. They waste hundreds of hours.

Al: There is lots of wasted time.

Tim: The best example I can think of—I remember doing this in my sophomore year. I was taking an American History course and everybody said, "Outline your books, use the yellow markers." I took a history book which was 700 and something pages. I outlined half of the entire book in preparation for the test. A big, gigantic history book. And halfway through I said to myself, "Are you crazy? What are you going to do with these outlines once you are done?" If you pick up a book on study skills, a lot of them say practice outlining the book. They suggest a lot of crazy things that, in fact, don't work. And I finally said, "Ugh! I'll never outline another book in my life." And I never did.

Al: So this is why, in our whole thing on student success, there has not once been any mention of taking a yellow marker or a ruler and underlining or highlighting the important words and phrases.

Tim: No! What do you have when it is all over? You've got a bunch of books that are underlined. How are you going to study? Go through the book and look at the important underlined things? . . . It can be all right if you want to

130

underline and circle answers to questions. I know people who do that. They say, "Here is an answer to a question." And I say, "Yes, the question was this and here is the answer." And they see they know the answer. That is one thing. Going through and circling or marking what you know are important answers to questions. But just to underline and underline every time you see another important point or outline notes because that is what you practice in school! Remember making outlines?

Al: Right. Some students use underlining to try to help pay attention to what they are reading. The only time I use a yellow marker is when I find a statement the author makes that I think I might come back and quote some day, or I want to be able to find the statement quickly, I'll use a yellow marker down the border or maybe to highlight some phrases in sentences, but I will only do this maybe two or three times in an entire book.

Tim: You have to make yourself ask whenever you do something like this, "How is this going to help me to do better on a test?" or "help me ask or answer an important question?" Many people suggest things to students, which if they ever did themselves, they would find out they were burdens and a waste of time. They're good things to do if you plan to spend twelve hours a day studying. You enjoy reading and rereading and going over outlines and underline pages, etc., etc. I am not saying you can't pick up the information that way, but it is very tough to put it all together. What happens is that you're very good at memorizing large bodies of information.

Al: Either that or you just practice recognition.

Tim: Right, and what's that good for? The best example I can give of how I realized how useless all that was was when I went home and got out two gigantic boxes of all the notes I took during my first two to three years of college. I browsed through them and I didn't recognize a thing. Why? Because all I did was practice outlining, remembering, and recognizing stuff. And, interestingly enough, after looking at my graduate notes, all those notes are familiar. They were all very important. They covered topics which I got to know very well. I am sure that is true with most people. You take your college notes and you could throw them out the door and never see them again and you haven't lost anything. People say, "Well, if you were forced to, you could remember that stuff and it would make it very meaningful." No, it wouldn't. It's meaningless information. I no more could tell you about the anthropology of American Indians or the geography of Australia than I could the day I entered the course. And I think that is tragic. An education is something you should be able to take with you.

Al. Well, you've got to acknowledge there is going to be a lot of forgetting that takes place no matter *what* approach you use.

Tim: Yes, but when I am to the point where I don't even know where Australia is on the map . . .

Al: (laughing) Come on, Tim!

Tim: . . . I couldn't tell you where the Navajo lived! . . . The point I am trying to get across to the students is, "Don't waste your time." Figure out where you want to go, how you're going to get there, and how you know you've arrived. At the end of the day, if you can't say, "I've accomplished this, this, and this and I have studied this, this, and this, and now I can do better in this course because I know this and I didn't know it when I started out the day," then you are wasting your time.

Al: I have to disagree with you on that, because I believe that it's an equally okay, valid, legitimate way to go through life, getting up each morning and following your curiosity. I'm not saying every morning, but some mornings. Tim, you just made a pretty tight statement, like at the end of *each* day say I accomplished this, this, and this.

Tim: Something good has happened. I can do this that I couldn't do before.

Al: I think people are better off if they have some more throwaway time, where they don't accomplish anything. In fact, the purpose of it is to not accomplish something. To have a day where you are not working or accomplishing anything.

Tim: But what you might accomplish is just the fact that you relax and do nothing and you know that is good for you. Some people can't even say at the end of the day, "Hey, I just sat and did nothing and it was good."

Al: For the person who does not do that *every* day.

Tim: For the person who does that every day, I think there may be some problems.

Al: Which gets us to what everyone of us runs into. That is, no matter what we are doing, there is going to be someone who comes along and is unhappy about it. If a person is very relaxed and casual and doesn't accomplish a whole lot, someone says, "Hey, you ought to accomplish more." With a person who is accomplishing an awful lot, someone says, "Hey, slow down. You ought to relax and not try to accomplish so much." There will always be someone wanting people to be different from however they are.

Tim: In essence, we are saying to students to be whatever they want to be. And if they want to be better students, here are some things that, if they do them, will help them get there. It's their choice. If they want to, fine; if they don't want to, they can sell the book back.

Al: No, they can't! How about saying they should sell their book to someone else!

Tim: I'll buy that!

FEEDBACK REQUEST

Do you have any study tips, comments, constructive criticism, or suggestions you would like to pass along to us? If so, please send them to us c/o:

> Psychology Editor,
> College Department
> Holt, Rinehart and Winston
> 383 Madison Avenue
> New York, N.Y. 10017

What did you find of most value in this book?

In what ways might it be improved?

Other comments:

ACKNOWLEDGMENTS

This book is the result of the contribution of many people . . .

The many unnamed educators whose striving for improvement made available the large body of knowledge that we drew from.

Professor Wilbert J. McKeachie, whose many years of dedicated effort to improve teaching and whose personal support of beginning instructors created an exciting growth atmosphere at the University of Michigan.

Professor James B. McConnell, who advised each of us during our respective graduate years and then arranged for the meshing of talents of two people from opposite disciplines and opposite shores.

Deborah Doty and other Holt editors, who saw the need for the book and guided its development.

The many students who used the early versions and gave us helpful feedback.

Beverly Walter and Joan Siebert, who gave us sustained support and many useful suggestions.

Our animal friends, whose involvement in the work on our desks kept us aware of how important it is to have time for friends.

Tim and Al